I'll Teach You To Talk Back... For Real

A Guide to Self-Talk to Challenge Your Internal Anxiety Monologues

Dr. Kevon Owen

STEADY PRESS

No part of this book may be reproduced, stored in a retrieval system, or transmitted in any form or by any means—electronic, mechanical, photocopying, recording, or otherwise—without the prior written permission of the publisher, except in the case of brief quotations used in reviews or scholarly works.

ISBN: 979-8-9929582-0-1
eBook ISBN: 979-8-9929582-1-8

Published by Steady Press

Cover illustration by Ali West

This book is not intended to provide medical, psychological, or legal advice. The content is for educational and inspirational purposes only and does not substitute for professional counseling, therapy, diagnosis, or treatment. If you are experiencing emotional or mental health difficulties, please seek the guidance of a qualified professional.

U.S. Copyright Office Registration Number: TXu-2-480-764

Printed in the United States of America.

First Edition

Copyright © 2025 Kevon Owen

All rights reserved.

Contents

1. Introduction: Welcome to Your Own Head — 1
2. PART 1: THE BAD NEWS – YOUR BRAIN CAN BE A JERK — 5
3. Chapter 1: The Lies We Believe (And Why They're So Convincing) — 6
4. Chapter 2: Anxiety — The Internal Drama Queen — 18
5. Chapter 3: Your Brain vs. Reality — 31
6. PART 2: THE GOOD NEWS – YOU CAN REWRITE THE SCRIPT — 47
7. Chapter 4: How to Respond When Your Brain is Misbehaving — 48
8. Chapter 5: The Science of Talking Back to Yourself — 60
9. Chapter 6: The Uncomfortable But Necessary Art of Self-Compassion — 74
10. PART 3: COPING STRATEGIES – BECAUSE YOU CAN'T JUST THINK YOUR WAY OUT OF EVERYTHING — 88
11. Chapter 7: Action > Anxiety — 89
12. Chapter 8: Externalizing the Crazy — 103
13. Chapter 9: The Power of the Absurd — 119
14. PART 4: LONG-TERM THINKING – CHANGING YOUR INNER MONOLOGUE FOR GOOD — 131
15. Chapter 10: Rewriting Your Mental Script (For Real This Time) — 132
16. Chapter 11: The Life-Changing Magic — 149
17. Chapter 12: The Final Word – You're Not Your Thoughts — 156
18. A Letter to All the Overthinkers — 168

Introduction: Welcome to Your Own Head

Congratulations, You Live with a Narrator Who Won't Shut Up

You're Not Crazy, You Just Think You Are

Let's clear something up right away: You're not crazy.

I mean, sure, you've had some interesting thoughts. You've probably imagined entire arguments in the shower that never happened. Maybe you've rehearsed your order in a drive-thru so many times that when the person said, "Welcome to Chick-fil-A," your brain panicked and you blurted out, "You too." Or perhaps you've spent hours lying awake at night, replaying that clumsy thing you did five years ago while your rational self screams, "IT DOESN'T MATTER!" but your anxiety is like, "Oh, it definitely matters. In fact, let's replay it in HD with director's commentary."

But having an internal monologue that occasionally spirals into nonsense doesn't make you crazy. It makes you human.

We all talk to ourselves. Some of us do it out loud (which alarms people in grocery stores), while the rest of us keep it inside, where it's just as chaotic but socially acceptable. This little voice in your head—your inner narrator—is constantly shaping your emotions, decisions, and confidence, whether you realize it or not. It's running commentary on everything. And sometimes, it's a jerk.

You know that friend who always assumes the worst? The one who hears "we need to talk" and immediately starts planning their funeral? Your brain is that friend. Your brain is the friend who sees you cough once and says, "Well, goodbye forever, it was nice knowing you." Your brain is the friend who watches you drop a glass and whispers, "This is why we can't have nice things, Janet."

The Daily Soundtrack of Your Mind

Imagine your self-talk as a playlist that's on constant repeat. Some days, it's pumping out bangers that make you feel unstoppable:

"I've got this!" "That meeting went better than I expected." "I handled that situation like a boss."

But other days? It's a collection of the most depressing songs you've ever heard:

"Why even try? You'll just mess it up again." "Everyone else has their life together. What's wrong with you?" "Remember that embarrassing thing from 2014? Let's think about it in excruciating detail! For the next three hours! While adding new, even more humiliating 'what if' scenarios!"

The kicker is that unlike an actual playlist, you can't just hit "skip" when a bad thought comes on. Instead, you get stuck in a mental loop, where one negative thought leads to another, and suddenly you're spiraling because someone didn't text you back within five minutes.

"They haven't texted back in six minutes. They must be ignoring me. They probably hate me now. I'm sure that last message I sent was weird. Actually, everything I've ever said to them has been weird. They're probably showing all their friends my texts right now and laughing. I should probably move to another country and change my name."

Seems reasonable, right?

How Self-Talk Shapes Anxiety, Confidence, and Life Itself

Your internal monologue has more power than you think. It can either be your biggest cheerleader or your worst critic. It can talk you into chasing your dreams or convince you that you're not good enough. It can remind you of everything you've accomplished or whisper, You're a fraud, and it's only a matter of time before people find out.

The problem is, most of us don't challenge our self-talk. We assume that because a thought pops into our head, it must be true.

Thought: "I just embarrassed myself. Now everyone thinks I'm an idiot." Reality: Everyone was too busy scrolling Instagram to notice.

Thought: "If I don't succeed at this, I'll be a total failure." Reality: Nobody actually has a perfect track record, and failure is how people learn.

Thought: "I need to respond to this text immediately, or they'll think I'm mad." Reality: Most people respond at random times because life is happening.

See what's happening here? Your brain is like a overreactiontic friend who jumps to conclusions without checking the facts. It means well, but it's not always reliable.

Your brain: "You have a headache? Probably a tumor."Reality: "You haven't had water in six hours and you're staring at a screen."

Psych Insight*Your brain sometimes acts like a faulty weather forecast, predicting storms on sunny days.*

Emotional Reasoning Note*Emotional reasoning is like believing your anxiety about flying means planes are objectively unsafe.*

Cognitive Distortion Alert*This thought illustrates the cognitive distortion of 'catastrophizing', an exaggerated perception of negative outcomes.*

Your brain: "They didn't laugh at your joke. Never speak again."Reality: "They didn't hear you over the restaurant noise."

Mind-Reading Analysis*Mind-reading anxiety is like assuming everyone is a harsh movie critic reviewing your every move.*

Personalization Note*Personalization—taking responsibility for things outside your control, like blaming yourself if it rains during your barbecue.*

Your brain: "You're going to bomb this presentation and your career will be over."Reality: "You're prepared, and even if you stumble, people will forget about it by lunchtime."

Emotional Reasoning Insight*Emotional reasoning is your brain thinking your feelings are facts—like believing a movie is scary because you jumped.*

Magnification Alert*This is like when you spill coffee and assume the whole day's ruined—magnification at its finest.*

Catastrophizing Note*This illustrates catastrophizing, a cognitive distortion of assuming worst-case outcomes.*

Why We Believe the Things We Tell Ourselves (Even When They're Clearly Dumb)

If someone else talked to you the way you talk to yourself, you'd probably tell them to take a hike. But because these thoughts are inside our own heads, we accept them without question.

Why?

Because our beliefs—especially the ones about ourselves—aren't just based on logic. They're built over time, like an unreliable Wikipedia page that random strangers keep editing. And those strangers? They're the experiences, people, and messages that shaped us growing up.

Some of these beliefs came from obvious places, like:

That one teacher who told you that you'd never amount to anything.

The time you were picked last for kickball and decided, Welp, guess I'm just not athletic.

That job interview where they said, "We're going in a different direction," and your brain translated it to, You are unhireable, unskilled, and should probably go live in a cave.

Other beliefs are sneakier. They come from years of small messages that seep into your subconscious:

Social media influencers subtly convincing you that your life isn't as exciting as it should be.

Watching your parents react to stress and accidentally absorbing their anxieties as your own.

Every romantic comedy where the only happy ending is finding true love, subtly telling you that if you're single, you're incomplete (spoiler: that's nonsense).

By the time we're adults, we've collected an entire set of core beliefs—many of them untrue, unhelpful, and totally unchecked.

PART 1: THE BAD NEWS – YOUR BRAIN CAN BE A JERK

Let's dive straight into the cold, hard truth: that three-pound organ sitting between your ears isn't always your best friend. In fact, sometimes it's the equivalent of that "friend" who tells you your haircut looks "interesting" and then posts an unflattering photo of you online. Your brain can be a total jerk—not because it's you, and not because it's out to get you, but because it's running prehistoric software in a digital world. Over the next three chapters, we'll explore exactly how your brain lies to you, why anxiety is the theatrics queen of emotions, and what happens when your thoughts go head-to-head with reality (spoiler alert: your thoughts usually lose, badly). Buckle up—we're about to meet the jerk who's been living rent-free in your head for far too long.

Chapter 1: The Lies We Believe (And Why They're So Convincing)

Why You Absolutely, 100% Need to Start Talking Back—For Real This Time

Let's start with the good news: Your brain is amazing. It keeps your heart beating, helps you remember where you left your car keys (most of the time), and can recall every lyric to that one song from the '90s that you haven't heard in years.

Now, the bad news: Your brain is also a master storyteller—and not always a truthful one. It's like if Stephen King and a pathological liar had a baby who grew up to write your internal monologue.

If you grew up in a household where "talking back" was a federal offense, then congratulations! You've been trained your whole life to stay silent when someone tells you nonsense—even if that someone is your own brain.

When we were kids, talking back to our parents usually resulted in some form of swift and decisive justice:

The Look. You know the one. That death stare that let you know you were on thin ice. The kind of look that made you wonder if your parents had secret laser vision they were holding back.

The "What Did You Just Say?" A question designed to make you reflect on every life choice you'd made up until that moment. A question that wasn't actually a question at all, but a chance for you to dig your own grave deeper.

The Swift Consequence. Maybe it was early bedtime. Maybe it was no dessert. Maybe it was a well-placed sandal (bless the accuracy of 90s moms everywhere, who could hit a moving target from thirty feet away with a flip-flop they'd removed in one fluid motion).

We were taught that respect meant not talking back. That when someone older, bigger, or louder than us spoke, we were supposed to just accept it and move on.

And I get it. That rule mostly makes sense in parenting. But do you know where it does not make sense?

In your own head.

Because let me tell you something: Your brain talks back to YOU all the time.

And most of the time? It is lying.

Here's the thing about your brain: it's got more audacity than a scam caller trying to reach you about your car's extended warranty. Your brain will tell you something absolutely ridiculous, with complete confidence, and then just move on like it didn't just emotionally dropkick you for no reason.

"Hey, just a quick reminder that everyone in that meeting was judging you when you stumbled over that one word. Anyway, what should we have for lunch?"

Your Brain: The Over Enthusiastic Screenwriter

Your brain is like an overenthusiastic screenwriter who never fact-checks their work but still insists that every script deserves an Oscar. And the movie it loves making the most? The Dramatic Misinterpretation of Your Life, starring You, with guest appearances by Anxiety and That One Embarrassing Memory from Middle School That Won't Die.

If you've ever convinced yourself that everyone at the party secretly hates you, or that one clumsy conversation means you'll die alone, congratulations! You've fallen victim to one of your brain's many creative reinterpretations of reality.

The real kicker? We believe these stories, no matter how absurd they are. Why? Because they don't show up as stories. They show up as truth. And when something feels true, we rarely stop to question it.

It's like when you wake up from a dream where your friend betrayed you, and you're mad at them in real life for a solid fifteen minutes. Your brain is like, "That definitely happened! I saw it with my own...imagination."

For example:

Your Brain: "Hey, quick heads-up. Everyone is secretly judging you right now."

Do we stop and say, "Excuse me, brain, where exactly are you getting this information? Do you have access to everyone's thoughts? Are you secretly Professor X? Did you take a poll?"

NO.

We just accept it.

Oh no. They are judging me. I am now in full social crisis mode. I should leave this party immediately and possibly change my name and move to another country.

Or how about this classic?

Your Brain: "You're a complete failure. You always mess up everything."

Do we push back and say, "Actually, I've succeeded at many things, and nobody always fails at everything, statistically speaking. That's just mathematically impossible. Even if I tried to fail at everything, I'd probably accidentally succeed at something."

NOPE.

We say, "Wow, great point, brain. I'll go ahead and spiral into self-loathing now. You're obviously the expert on my life, despite consistently giving me terrible advice."

SEE THE PROBLEM HERE?

For years, we were told, Don't talk back. But now?

Oh, friend. Now it is time.

Now it is time to raise an eyebrow at your brain and say, "Citations needed."

The Big Lies We Tell Ourselves

So let's talk about some of the biggest lies we tell ourselves—and, more importantly, how to start talking back.

Lie #1: "I'm Not Good Enough."

(Also known as: "I need to be more successful, attractive, interesting, talented, productive, or possibly taller.")

You know that feeling when you're doing just fine in life—maybe even thriving—and then suddenly, some small thing sets off a mental avalanche of self-doubt?

Let's say you're at work, and your boss walks by without saying hello. Your brain immediately launches into:

They're mad at me.

I must have screwed something up.

I knew it. I don't belong here. I'm a fraud, and at any moment, I'm going to be escorted out of the building in shame, possibly with a cardboard box containing my sad desk plant and that half-eaten granola bar I was saving for later.

Reality check: Your boss was probably just thinking about their lunch order. Or maybe they were mentally rehearsing a conversation with their teenager who just asked to borrow the car. Or perhaps they're just constipated. But your brain? It turns a two-second non-event into evidence that you are failing at life.

It's like interpreting someone not waving back at you as proof that you should never leave your house again, when they were just fumbling for their keys or thinking about whether they turned off the stove.

Where This Lie Comes From:

This belief usually starts in childhood. Maybe you had high expectations placed on you. Maybe you were praised for being "the smart one" or "the responsible one," and now, anything less than amazing feels like failure. Maybe you got the message that who you are isn't quite enough—that you have to prove your worth through achievement, approval, or productivity.

Or maybe you just watched too many Disney movies where the main character has to learn some extraordinary skill, save the kingdom, and get the perfect partner, all while maintaining immaculate hair. No pressure.

How to Talk Back to It:

Fact-Check Your Brain. Ask yourself: Says who? Where is the official "You're Not Enough" certification, and why haven't they mailed it to you? (Hint: Because it doesn't exist.) Is there a "good enough" inspection team I don't know about? Did someone leave a clipboard with my life assessment that I missed?

Stop Moving the Goalposts. If you're constantly telling yourself, I'll be enough when I accomplish [insert impossible standard here], then you're playing a game you can't win. "I'll be enough when I get the promotion." *gets promotion* "I'll be enough when I buy a house." *buys house* "I'll be enough when I renovate the kitchen." It never ends. It's like trying to reach the horizon—it keeps moving as you approach it.

Try the "Best Friend Test." If your best friend told you, "I feel like I'm not enough," what would you say? Would you list all the reasons they're inadequate? Or would you remind them of their value beyond their achievements? Now say that same thing to yourself. Unless you're a terrible friend, in which case maybe get a new perspective.

Lie #2: "Everyone is Judging Me."

(Or: "All eyes are on me, and every mistake I make will be analyzed like the Zapruder film.")

Ever left a conversation and thought, Did I talk too much? Did I say something dumb? Are they secretly annoyed by me? Is there a committee meeting right now where they're voting on whether to ever speak to me again?

Or maybe you tripped on a crack in the sidewalk, and your brain screamed, EVERYONE SAW! YOU'RE A PUBLIC DISGRACE! PEOPLE ARE ALREADY CREATING MEMES ABOUT YOU!

Here's the truth: People aren't thinking about you nearly as much as you think they are. Not because you're not important, but because they're too busy overanalyzing their own lives.

It's called the spotlight effect—the psychological phenomenon where we believe that people are paying way more attention to us than they actually are. It should really be called the "main character syndrome," where we think we're the star of everyone else's show, when really we're lucky if we get a cameo.

Plausible Scenario:

Meet Kara. Kara goes to a party and makes a joke that doesn't quite land. The second it leaves her mouth, she feels it: the dreaded social uncomfortableness heat wave. Her brain starts spiraling.

Oh no, they didn't laugh. Do they think I'm weird?

They probably regret inviting me.

This is exactly why I should stay home and just text my cat.

I need to leave immediately and possibly fake my own death.

Meanwhile, here's what actually happened: One person was distracted by their phone. Another was wondering if there was guacamole at the snack table. And the rest of the group forgot about the joke approximately 0.3 seconds after she said it because they were all too busy worried about whether their own last comment was weird.

That's the irony: everyone is too worried about themselves to worry about you. It's like a room full of people all thinking, "Everyone is looking at me!" while looking at no one.

CHAPTER 1: THE LIES WE BELIEVE (AND WHY THEY'RE SO CONVINCING) 11

How to Talk Back to It:

The "What Were They Wearing?" Test. Try to remember what your coworker wore three days ago. Can't? That's how much they're paying attention to you. Humans are notoriously self-absorbed creatures. We're all starring in the movie of our own lives, which means everyone else is just a supporting character at best.

Flip the Script. Assume the best instead of the worst. What if they actually liked what you said? What if they were too preoccupied with their own self-doubt to notice your clumsy moment? What if—and this is revolutionary—nobody cares as much as you think they do?

Adopt the "So What?" Mindset. So what if you said something weird? Will it matter in five days? Five months? Five years? Exactly. In the grand timeline of your life, this moment is a blip. In the grand timeline of the universe, it's not even that. You think the cosmos cares about that time you called your teacher "Mom" in third grade? (Though to be fair, the kids in your class might remember that one for a while.)

Lie #3: "If I'm Not Perfect, I've Failed."

(Or: "Anything less than an A+ is a disgrace to my ancestors.")

Perfectionism is sneaky. It pretends to be ambition, but really, it's fear in disguise.

It's why you procrastinate on writing that report because you're scared it won't be good enough. It's why you don't try new things—because what if you're bad at them? It's why you'd rather send a text like, "Hey, sorry, I've been super busy!" instead of admitting you just forgot to respond for three days because you were binge-watching renovation shows and eating cereal out of the box.

It's like having a really strict internal teacher who gives you an F if you get a 99% instead of 100%. That's not a high standard; that's just mean.

Where This Lie Comes From:

Maybe you grew up in an environment where mistakes weren't tolerated.

Maybe you got praised only when you achieved something.

Maybe you just really, really hate being wrong. (Though, let's be honest, who enjoys it? "Oh boy, I can't wait to be completely incorrect today!")

Maybe you watched too many sports movies where the protagonist trains montage-style and then wins the big championship. Not as many movies show the protagonist coming in fourth place and saying, "Well, I tried my best and had fun."

How to Talk Back to It:

"Done is Better Than Perfect." That novel you haven't started? The email you haven't sent? The gym membership you refuse to use until you're already in shape? Perfection keeps you stuck. It's like refusing to get in the pool until you know how to swim.

Set a "Good Enough" Goal. Instead of "I have to work out five times a week or I'm a failure," try "I'll move my body three times this week." Instead of "This has to be the best presentation ever given in the history of the company," try "This needs to effectively convey the main points."

Remind Yourself: No One Else is Perfect. The most successful people? They've failed a lot. The only difference is they kept going anyway. Did you know that Oprah was fired from her first TV job? That Stephen King's first novel was rejected 30 times? That Michael Jordan didn't make his high school basketball team? Success isn't about never failing; it's about getting back up.

Learning to Talk Back (The Right Way)

The alternative to talking back to your brain is internal repression and a verbal thrashing like none other.

And let me tell you something: Your anxiety is more than happy to be in charge.

Anxiety doesn't whisper, "Hey, quick question, do you maybe want to be worried about this?"

No. It barges in. It takes over. It drops a terrible thought bomb into your head and expects you to just sit there and accept it. Anxiety doesn't knock on the door; it kicks it down while wearing a SWAT team outfit and yelling through a megaphone.

Imagine if your anxiety were an actual person. Let's call them Skippy.

Skippy shows up out of nowhere and says:

"Hey, remember that super embarrassing thing you did 12 years ago? Let's relive it in HD! I've added surround sound and slow-motion replay for the really cringy parts!"

"Oh wow, your stomach hurts. You're probably dying. We should Google this immediately. In fact, let's check WebMD and pick out a casket while we're online."

"That text message was suspiciously short. Your friend definitely hates you now. They've already deleted your contact and are telling everyone what a terrible person you are."

"Did you hear that noise in your house? It's either a serial killer, a ghost, or a serial killer ghost. There are no other possibilities."

Would you just let Skippy say this stuff and not push back?

NO! You would tell Skippy to sit down, take a deep breath, and maybe seek professional help. You'd say, "Skippy, I appreciate your concern, but you have the risk assessment skills of a squirrel on espresso."

That is exactly what we need to do with our internal anxiety monologues.

How to Start Talking Back

I am about to teach you the fine art of talking back to your brain.

You are going to challenge those thoughts the way an attorney tears apart a witness on the stand. You are going to argue with your anxiety like it just tried to cut in front of you in a drive-thru line when you've been waiting for 20 minutes and they only have three cars.

You are going to stop accepting nonsense thoughts as truth.

And it all starts with these simple steps:

Step 1: Treat Your Thoughts Like Unverified Gossip.

If someone ran up to you and breathlessly said, "Oh my, did you hear that EVERYONE at work secretly hates you?" would you believe them instantly?

No! You'd fact-check that garbage. You'd say, "That seems unlikely. Who told you that? Where's your evidence? Are you just making this up because I didn't share my fries with you earlier?"

So next time your brain drops a melodramatic headline like "You're a total failure and no one likes you," respond accordingly:

"Oh yeah? WHO SAID THAT? WHERE IS YOUR SOURCE? Let me speak to your editor because this reporting is shoddy at best."

"That's interesting. Is this peer-reviewed information, or are you just making stuff up again?"

"Are we reading from the same book of facts? Because that doesn't sound factual to me."

Step 2: Start Asking, "Says Who?"

Your brain: "Congratulations, you forgot your reusable grocery bag. you've disappointed an imaginary environmental council of judgmental penguins in you, and dolphins everywhere have unanimously disowned you."

You: "Says who? Show me the evidence. Is there a written report I can reference? Has there been a formal evaluation that I wasn't invited to? Did the Council of Good Enough People meet and vote on this?"

PSYCH NOTE: *Personalization is assuming responsibility for everything, like thinking traffic jams are personally targeting your commute.*

Your brain: "Everyone is judging you right now."

You: "Oh really? Did you survey the room? Where's the data? Show me the pie chart, Skippy. I want to see the demographics of this judging. What percentage is actively judging versus those who are thinking about their grocery lists or wondering if they left the oven on?"

Your brain: "You're going to fail this test/presentation/conversation/life."

You: "Based on what evidence? My actual track record of handling similar situations, or your weird fixation with worst-case scenarios? Because historically, Skippy, your predictions have been about as accurate as a weather forecast two months in advance."

NOTE: *Mind-reading anxiety is like assuming everyone is a harsh movie critic reviewing your every move.*

Step 3: Give Your Anxiety the Same Energy You'd Give a Pushy Salesperson.

Your brain: "You should absolutely panic about this thing that is probably not a big deal."

You: "Ooooh, you ALMOST got me. That was a good pitch. Very melodramatic. Love the urgency. But I'm gonna have to go ahead and say NOPE. Thanks for stopping by though! Maybe try again with a more reasonable suggestion."

INSIGHT: *Emotional reasoning is your brain thinking your feelings are facts—like believing a movie is scary because you jumped.*

Treat your anxiety like that overly aggressive salesperson at the mall kiosk who tries to put lotion on your hands without permission. A firm "No thank you, I'm not interested in catastrophic thinking today" works wonders.

Step 4: When in Doubt, Be Ridiculous.

One of the best ways to disarm anxiety is to mock it a little. Take its extremely serious, doom-filled pronouncements and make them so over-the-top that they become absurd.

For example:

Your brain: "What if that mole on your arm is something serious?"

NOTE: *Personalization—taking responsibility for things outside your control, like blaming yourself if it rains during your barbecue.*

You: "You're right. I am the first person in medical history to be diagnosed with Instantaneous Rare Mole Disease. Tragic. They'll probably name it after me. Future medical students will study my case for centuries to come. 'And here we have the Jones Mole Phenomenon, the only case in which a completely normal mole caused someone's entire life to implode within hours.'"

Or:

Your brain: "You're going to fail this presentation and your career will be over."

You: "Yes, because one PowerPoint mishap will absolutely send my entire life into ruin. This is definitely how things work. In fact, they'll probably create a new company policy named after me. 'Let's not pull a [your name] in this presentation.' They'll add a section about me to the employee handbook and use my picture as a warning to others."

Your brain is overreactiontic. Treat it like it's being dramatic. When your anxiety is determined to throw a five-alarm fire over a candle, it's okay to bring a water gun to the fight and say, "Is this what you wanted? Is this proportional enough for you?"

Your Thoughts Aren't the Boss of You

Listen, I get it. Your thoughts feel real. And some of them? They're important. Some thoughts are like that friend who tells you there's spinach in your teeth before a big meeting. Thank you, helpful thought!

But not all thoughts deserve a seat at the table. Some thoughts are like that friend who texts you at 2 AM with "Are you awake? I just had a thought about how whales might get lonely. Do you think whales have best friends? What if their best friend swims away and they can't find them again?"

Some thoughts? Some thoughts need to go sit in the corner and think about what they've done.

Your brain will offer up some truly ridiculous ideas. Your job? Talk back.

You do not have to believe every thought that enters your head. You do not have to treat every anxious spiral like it's breaking news. You don't have to accept your brain's first draft as the final version.

You get to rewrite the script.

And it starts with something as simple as recognizing, Hey, maybe my brain is just being melodramatic today.

So if you've spent your life being told not to talk back, I'm telling you right now: It is time to talk back.

Because the alternative? The alternative is letting Skippy (your internal monologue) run wild, unchecked, making every small inconvenience feel like the end of the world.

And we're not doing that anymore.

Because at the end of the day? You're doing just fine. You're reading a book about improving your mental health, which means you're self-aware and working on yourself. That's already more than many people do.

Your brain might be a melodrama queen, but you? You're the director of this show. It's time to take control of the script.

Chapter 2: Anxiety — The Internal Drama Queen

And How to Put Her in Her Place (Wow, That Escalated Quickly.)

If you've ever had a friend who overreacts to everything, then congratulations—you already understand how anxiety works.

You know that person who gets one vague email from their boss and immediately assumes they're about to get fired, lose their house, and have to move into a cardboard box? Or the one who coughs one time and suddenly they're googling rare diseases and mentally planning their own funeral? ("I'd like 'Another One Bites the Dust' played ironically at my service, and please make sure my cat gets therapy.")

That's anxiety. Drama. Queen.

Anxiety is that person in a movie who gasps loudly at the slightest noise. It's the friend who texts "EMERGENCY!!!" and when you call back panicking, they tell you they can't decide which shoes to wear. It's the overenthusiastic narrator in your head who takes the smallest situation and turns it into a multi-episode theatrics series with guest appearances by Worst-Case Scenario and Sudden Existential Crisis.

"What's that? You have a presentation tomorrow? Let me set the scene: You'll wake up late because your alarm didn't go off. Your car won't start. When you finally arrive, sweaty and disheveled, you'll forget everything you prepared. People will laugh. Your boss will fire you on the spot. You'll become homeless. Eventually, archaeologists will find your remains centuries later and use you as an example of 'career failure in the early 21st century.'"

And because this is happening inside your head, it feels true. It feels like the absolute, indisputable gospel truth, delivered directly to your brain by the universe itself. Not a suggestion. Not a possibility. A FACT.

So today? We're putting anxiety in her place. We're taking away her megaphone, canceling her Netflix special, and reminding her that she is not, in fact, the director of your life story.

Meet Anxiety: The Overenthusiastic, Uninvited Party Guest

Anxiety means well. She thinks she's helping. She thinks she's protecting you from disaster. She thinks she's being useful.

But much like an over-caffeinated relative with a bullhorn, she does not know when to stop.

Her job is supposed to be warning you about actual danger. But instead of just nudging you when you're about to step into traffic, she alerts you constantly, theatrically, and often about things that aren't even remotely dangerous.

It's like having a smoke detector that goes off when you're cooking, when you're showering, when you're sleeping, when a dust particle floats by, and occasionally, when there's actual smoke. After a while, you start to wonder if you should just take the batteries out (please don't—this metaphor has limits, and also fire safety is important).

Anxiety is that friend who watches one true crime documentary and then calls you at 3 AM convinced there's a serial killer outside their window, when it's just the neighbor's cat knocking over a trash can.

Let's compare:

When Anxiety is Actually Helpful:

"Hey, you should wear a seatbelt."

"Maybe don't text your ex. That's a bad idea. Remember last time when you ended up drunk-ordering $200 worth of cheese online?"

"That dark alley seems sketchy. Let's take another route, preferably one with streetlights and fewer mysterious figures lurking in shadows."

"This person is giving off some serious red flags. Maybe reconsider this relationship before you end up as the subject of a true crime podcast."

Okay, Anxiety, I see you. Solid points. Good hustle. In these scenarios, anxiety is that friend who stops you from making truly terrible decisions, the one who holds your hair back when you've had too much to drink and whispers, "I told you so," but then hands you a glass of water anyway.

When Anxiety is Absolutely Out of Control:

"Hey, you just said 'you too' to the waiter when they told you to enjoy your meal. Let's think about that forever. In fact, let's create a detailed timeline of every uncomfortable thing you've ever said to service workers going back to 2003."

"You haven't heard from your best friend in six hours. That means they're mad at you and plotting their escape from your life. They've probably already formed a new friend group specifically designed to exclude you."

"Your stomach hurts a little. This is it. It was nice knowing you. Should we call your parents now or write them a heartfelt goodbye letter?"

"Everyone at this party is secretly judging your outfit. They're all fashion experts, apparently. Anna Wintour is hiding in the kitchen just to get material for a scathing editorial about your sock choice."

"That meeting went fine, but did you notice how your boss looked at you when you mentioned that idea? CAREER OVER. Start practicing saying 'Would you like fries with that?'"

"Your child is five minutes late coming home from school. Time to imagine every possible tragedy that could have befallen them in excruciating detail! I've prepared a PowerPoint presentation with color-coded scenarios ranging from 'mild danger' to 'plots of horror movies that are somehow now reality.'"

Excuse me, Anxiety? WHAT ARE YOU EVEN TALKING ABOUT?

But do we push back? No.

We just accept these thoughts like they're facts.

We let them bully us into spiraling, overthinking, and doubting ourselves.

This is like letting that one theatrical friend plan your entire vacation because they once read an article about a hotel disaster in 2003. "We can't stay there! Don't you know what could happen?! I read about a person who found a hair in their hotel shower! A HAIR! We could all be dead by morning!"

So let's fix that. Let's reclaim our mental real estate from this overthinking squatter who's been living rent-free in our heads for far too long.

The Anxiety Spiral: How One Tiny Thought Becomes an Emotional Hurricane

Before we dive into solutions, let's take a moment to appreciate the artistic genius of anxiety—the way it can take one harmless thought and transform it into a full-blown emotional crisis in 3.5 seconds flat. Anxiety could turn "we need more milk" into an existential crisis faster than you can say "dairy alternative."

Let's watch this process unfold:

Step 1: The Trigger Your phone buzzes. It's a text from your spouse: "We need to talk."

Step 2: The Initial Thought "Hmm, I wonder what they want to talk about."

Step 3: Anxiety Enters the Chat "They're breaking up with you." (Anxiety doesn't ease into conversations. It kicks down the door like it's leading a police raid.)

Step 4: You Try to Be Reasonable "That seems extreme. Maybe they just want to discuss weekend plans."

Step 5: Anxiety Doubles Down "No, it's definitely a breakup. Remember how they seemed a little distant yesterday? And how they didn't laugh as hard at your joke? And how they chose strawberry ice cream when they KNOW you prefer chocolate? They've been planning this for weeks. Possibly months. They probably have a spreadsheet of all your flaws organized by category."

Step 6: The Spiral Accelerates "Oh good, they're leaving me. I'll be alone forever. I'll have to move out. I'll have to cancel that vacation we planned. I'll have to tell everyone we broke up. My parents will be so disappointed. I'll die alone surrounded by cats who will probably eat my face when I'm gone. Do cats even like faces? I should google that. No wait, I should focus on my impending doom."

Step 7: Complete Emotional Meltdown All of this happens before you even reply to the text, which, when answered, turns out to be: "We need to talk about what to have for dinner because I'm starving."

The most infuriating part? This entire apocalyptic scenario took place entirely in your head, took years off your life through stress, and was based on absolutely nothing.

If anxiety were a carnival ride, it would be called "The Ridiculous Leap to Conclusions" and there would be a sign saying "You must be this neurotic to ride."

Step 1: Recognizing When Anxiety is Being Ridiculous

The first thing we need to do is recognize when anxiety is lying to us.

Anxiety likes to present itself as FACT. No evidence. No citations. Just straight-up panic and nonsense. It's like a tabloid newspaper published directly in your brain: "DISASTER IMMINENT, SOURCES SAY." When you ask what sources, anxiety mumbles something about "people are saying" and changes the subject.

So let's play a game: "Actual Problem or Just Anxiety Being Dramatic?"

Scenario 1: Your Boss Sends You an Email That Just Says, "We Need to Talk."

What Anxiety Tells You: You committed some sort of workplace crime and are about to be escorted out in disgrace. Your career is over. You'll never work in this industry again. Time to update your resume and possibly consider a new identity in another country. Maybe you should start researching how to live off the grid. Can you grow your own food? Do you have survival skills? Should you start hoarding canned goods now?

Probable Reality: Your boss wants to know if you can cover a meeting on Friday, discuss that new project, or maybe even—gasp—give you positive feedback about something you did well. Maybe they just want to know if you've seen their stapler.

Scenario 2: Your Friend Hasn't Texted You Back All Day.

What Anxiety Tells You: You deeply offended them, they hate you now, and you will be friendless forever. Everything you said in your last conversation is being dissected and judged. They're probably showing your texts to other friends and laughing. They've created a group chat specifically to discuss how awful you are. You should just never text anyone again. In fact, throw your phone into the sea and move to a monastery where vows of silence are mandatory.

Probable Reality: They got busy, lost their phone, or (more likely) just forgot. Maybe they're taking a much-needed break from their phone. Maybe they're napping. Maybe the notification got buried under 47 other alerts. Maybe they started to reply, got distracted by a funny dog video, and completely forgot they were in the middle of texting you. Maybe—and this is revolutionary—it has absolutely nothing to do with you.

Scenario 3: You Feel a Weird Pain in Your Side.

What Anxiety Tells You: You have been stabbed and require immediate medical attention. Or worse, it's some rare disease that only three people in history have ever had, and all of them were diagnosed too late. You can practically hear the somber voice of the medical documentary narrator: "Little did they know, this slight discomfort was actually the first sign of..." You should immediately Google your symptoms and diagnose yourself based on the most catastrophic possibilities available on WebMD. Update your will while you're at it.

Probable Reality: You slept in a weird position. Or you're gassy. Or you pulled a muscle picking up a pen. Or you're just a human being who occasionally feels random bodily sensations that mean absolutely nothing. Bodies are weird and make random pains sometimes. It's like living in a house with old plumbing—sometimes it makes strange noises, but it doesn't mean the whole structure is about to collapse.

Scenario 4: You Make a Small Mistake at Work

What Anxiety Tells You: Everyone noticed. Your reputation is shattered. Your colleagues are whispering about your incompetence. Your boss is updating your performance review as we speak. The mistake will appear on every future reference check for the rest of your career. There's probably already a company-wide email thread titled "Can You Believe What They Did?" with your mistake detailed in bulleted lists. You might as well pack up your desk now.

Probable Reality: Either no one noticed or they noticed and immediately forgot because they're too wrapped up in their own lives and mistakes to catalog yours. People are remarkably forgiving of small errors because—surprise!—they make them too. In fact, they're probably too busy worrying about their own mistakes to even register yours. Remember when your coworker sent that email with a typo last month? No? Exactly.

Most of the time? It's anxiety being theatrical. Like, Broadway-musical-jazz-hands-and-kick-line dramatic. Like, someone-gave-a-teenager-twelve-energy-drinks-and-told-them-to-direct-a-soap-opera dramatic. Like Shakespeare-tragedy-where-everyone-dies-at-the-end dramatic, except the thing you're worried about is whether your email had the right tone.

The goal isn't to eliminate anxiety (because let's be honest, that's not happening). The goal is to stop believing everything it says. To recognize when it's going off the rails and say, "Thanks for your input, but maybe dial it back a few notches. Actually, dial it back all the notches."

Step 2: The "Shut Up, Skippy" Method

Sometimes, it helps to name your anxiety and treat it like an annoying person who just won't stop talking.

Let's call him Skippy.

Skippy is that guy at work who has opinions about everything but no actual expertise. Skippy always thinks the worst is about to happen. Skippy turns the smallest thing into a full-blown crisis. Skippy is the person at the meeting who turns a five-minute agenda item into a forty-five-minute debate.

Skippy barges into your mental office without knocking and starts spouting off about disasters that haven't happened, problems that don't exist, and scenarios he's entirely invented. Skippy has never been right about anything, ever, but he speaks with the confidence of someone who has never been wrong.

Picture Skippy wearing a tacky tie, holding a massive coffee mug that says "Worry Warrior," and using phrases like "just playing devil's advocate" and "well, actually" a lot.

Let's apply this:

Your brain: "Oh no, that mole looks weird. You should Google it and panic immediately. It's probably cancer. Or a spider egg sac that's about to hatch under your skin. Either way, you're doomed. Should we put together a farewell video montage now or wait until the diagnosis?"

You: "Shut up, Skippy. You're not a doctor. You've never been to medical school. You once convinced me I had a brain tumor, and it turned out to be a headache from not drinking enough water. Your medical opinions have all the credibility of a wellness influencer trying to sell magical healing crystals on Instagram."

Your brain: "Your friend didn't text back. Maybe they secretly can't stand you. Maybe they've been talking about you behind your back for years. Maybe your entire friendship has been a lie. Maybe they're plotting with your other friends to phase you out of the group. Maybe they've created an elaborate spreadsheet documenting all the reasons they can't stand you."

You: "Shut up, Skippy. People have lives. Remember when you said the same thing last month and then they texted back saying they were just busy with work? Maybe consider finding a hobby instead of inventing friendship catastrophes. Seriously, take up knitting or something. Make yourself useful."

Your brain: "That one clumsy thing you did five years ago? Yeah, people still remember it. They bring it up at parties when you're not there. It's probably mentioned in your obituary. 'Here lies [your name], who once mistook their boss for a waiter at a company dinner and asked them to bring more bread.'"

You: "SHUT. UP. Skippy. Nobody cares about that but you. Literally nobody. You're the only one with that mental highlight reel. Everyone else is too busy worrying about their own embarrassing moments that nobody else remembers either. It's like everyone's running around with their own personal Skippy. Nobody has time to remember my clumsy moments when they're too busy cringing about their own."

Skippy is not qualified to run your life. He is not credible. He has a terrible track record of predictions, and honestly, his anxiety forecasts have a worse success rate than a meteorologist trying to predict the weather six months in advance.

Tell him to pipe down. Put him on mute. Send him to voicemail. He's the spam caller of your mental space, and you don't have to pick up every time he rings. You can let his call go straight to voicemail, then delete without listening.

Step 3: Challenge the Thought Like a Lawyer in Court

If Skippy won't shut up, then it's time to cross-examine him like a witness in court. Put him on the stand and make him defend his ridiculous claims under oath. Channel your inner Law & Order prosecutor and make that anxious thought sweat.

Let's take a classic anxious thought:

Anxiety says: "If I mess up this presentation, everyone will think I'm incompetent, and I'll probably lose my job."

You (as the lawyer):

"Let's examine the evidence, Skippy. Have I ever done a presentation before?"

"Did I get fired last time?"

"Have I ever seen anyone get fired over one slightly uncomfortable presentation? Has the company ever called security to escort someone out because they fumbled a slide transition? Is there a clause in my contract that says 'One PowerPoint error = Immediate Termination'?"

"Do people usually get fired over one slightly clumsy presentation, or is that just something that happens in your anxiety fanfiction?"

"Wouldn't people more likely forget it ever happened within approximately 24 hours? Aren't they too busy thinking about their own presentations, their own work, and what they're having for lunch to dwell on my minor mistakes?"

"Can you name a single person who was immediately fired for a single imperfect presentation? Just one? With documentation? With witnesses? With a firing squad waiting outside the conference room?"

"If my colleague made a small mistake in a presentation, would I think they should be fired? Or would I barely notice and immediately go back to thinking about lunch? When Jessica stumbled over her words last week, did anyone care? Did the CEO burst through the wall like the Kool-Aid Man shouting 'YOU'RE FIRED'?"

If Skippy can't provide actual proof, his argument is dismissed. And spoiler alert: Skippy never has proof. Skippy has anxiety-fueled speculation masquerading as facts. Skippy has catastrophic fan fiction about your life, not evidence. Skippy is writing the screenplay for a disaster movie that's never going to be filmed.

Anxiety thrives on vague, ominous threats like:

"Everyone will hate me." (Who is everyone? All 7.9 billion people on Earth? The entire company? The room? The three people who actually matter in this situation?)

"This will ruin everything." (Everything? Your entire life? The fabric of space and time? The universe itself?)

"I can't handle this." (Based on what evidence? Your track record of surviving 100% of your bad days so far?)

"Everything will fall apart." (What constitutes "everything" here? Are we talking about your life or are we talking about molecular bonds?)

"I'll never recover from this." (Never? For the rest of your life? You'll be 97 years old in a nursing home still devastated about this Zoom call?)

"People will judge me forever." (Forever is a very long time. Are people really going to be on their deathbeds thinking about that time you said the wrong thing in a meeting?)

These sound scary—but they fall apart under questioning. They're the monster under the bed that disappears when you turn on the light and look closely. They're the strange noise in the night that turns out to be the refrigerator ice maker.

Ask yourself:

Is this thought actually true, or just my anxiety talking? Is this a fact or just a feeling dressed up as a fact?

What's the actual, real-world evidence that this will happen? Not what my anxiety is telling me might happen, but what has actually happened in similar situations.

How would I respond if my best friend had this thought? Would I agree with them or would I tell them they're being way too hard on themselves?

What's my actual track record with situations like this? Have I survived similar things before? (Spoiler alert: You have. You've survived 100% of your bad days so far.)

Six months from now, will this still matter? A year? Five years? Will this make it into the highlight reel of my life, or is it just a random Tuesday that no one will remember?

If this actually happened, would it truly be as catastrophic as I'm imagining? Is this actually the end of the world, or just a temporarily uncomfortable situation?

The minute you challenge a overreactive thought, it loses its grip. It's like a schoolyard bully who backs down the moment someone stands up to them. Anxiety is counting on you to just accept its wild claims without question. The moment you push back, it starts to crumble.

It's like in The Wizard of Oz when they finally pull back the curtain and find out it's just a small man with a microphone. Your anxiety is impressive and scary right up until the moment you examine it closely.

Step 4: What's the Worst That Could Happen?

Anxiety loves vague, ominous threats like "this will be a disaster." So when you define the disaster, it usually sounds... dumb. Like, embarrassingly dumb. Like, "why was I even worried about this?" dumb.

Your brain: "What if you make a mistake and it ruins your whole life?"

You: "Okay, walk me through exactly how that happens, Skippy. Step by step. I want a detailed roadmap from a single mistake to my entire life being ruined. Be specific. I want times, dates, and a cause-and-effect sequence that would hold up to peer review."

Nine times out of ten? It doesn't hold up. It's like a movie plot that falls apart as soon as you think about it for more than three seconds. "Wait, so the villain's entire plan depended on the hero being in exactly the right place at the right time with no contingency plan? That's just bad planning."

Take a moment to play out the absolute worst-case scenario. Really go there. And then ask:

"Would I survive this?" (Yes, because you're not actually in a Final Destination movie.)

"Have other people survived similar situations?" (Yes, because the world is full of people who have made mistakes and lived to tell about it.)

"Do I have any skills, resources, or support that would help me through this?" (Yes, because you're not actually alone on a desert island with nothing but your anxiety for company.)

"Have I weathered difficult situations before?" (Yes, because you're still here reading this book, which means you've survived everything life has thrown at you so far.)

Usually, the answer to all of these is yes. And suddenly, even the worst-case scenario—while not pleasant—becomes something you could handle. Not the end of the world. Not a complete catastrophe. Just a difficult situation that you would manage and move past, like countless other humans before you.

And let's be honest, how often does the absolute worst-case scenario actually happen? Almost never. We waste so much mental energy preparing for disasters that never arrive, catastrophes that never materialize, and judgments that never occur. It's like packing a winter coat, snow boots, and thermal underwear for a trip to Hawaii in July. Just in case there's a freak blizzard. In the tropics. In summer.

Step 5: Remember Your Anxiety's Greatest Hits (That Never Happened)

One of the most powerful ways to put anxiety in its place is to remember all the times it was catastrophically, embarrassingly wrong.

Start keeping a "Skippy's Failed Predictions" log. Every time anxiety tells you something terrible is about to happen, write it down. Then, when the situation resolves (and it almost always resolves just fine), write down what actually happened.

Over time, you'll build an impressive record of anxiety's terrible track record. Evidence that this voice in your head is about as reliable as a gossip columnist with a severe caffeine addiction.

For example:

What Skippy Predicted: "If you ask for a raise, your boss will think you're greedy and fire you." **What Actually Happened:** Got the raise with no theatrics whatsoever. Boss actually said, "I've been meaning to talk to you about this."

What Skippy Predicted: "That headache is definitely a brain tumor." **What Actually Happened:** It was dehydration. Again. Maybe try drinking water before WebMD next time.

What Skippy Predicted: "Everyone at the party will think you're clumsy and boring." **What Actually Happened:** Had three good conversations and no one seemed to be silently judging me. Someone even asked for my contact info to get coffee later.

What Skippy Predicted: "Your friend is mad at you because their text seemed short." **What Actually Happened:** They were just busy and everything was completely fine. They were actually texting from a meeting and trying not to get caught.

When you start documenting anxiety's failures, you begin to see the pattern: it's almost always wrong. And when you know someone has a history of being wrong, you stop taking their advice so seriously. You wouldn't keep going to a psychic who told you you'd meet your soulmate on Tuesday and then Tuesday comes and goes and the only contact you had with another human was the delivery person leaving your food on the porch.

Anxiety is a Liar, and You Don't Have to Listen

Look, anxiety isn't going anywhere. It's like that relative who always shows up for family gatherings uninvited. You can't stop it from arriving, but you don't have to give it the best seat at the table, and you certainly don't have to treat it like the guest of honor.

The difference between living with anxiety and being controlled by anxiety is learning when to call it out, challenge it, and refuse to let it run the show. It's about recognizing that just because something feels true doesn't mean it is true. Just because something is loud doesn't mean it's right.

Anxiety is the background character in your life story who keeps trying to steal the spotlight. It's time to remind it of its proper place—an occasional voice, not the narrator, not the director, and certainly not the star.

It's like that extra who keeps trying to get in every shot, and you need to kindly but firmly escort them back to where they belong. "Thanks for your enthusiasm, but this scene isn't about you."

From now on, when anxiety starts running its mouth, don't just sit there and take it.

Talk back. Challenge it. Mock it, even. Treat it like the unreliable, overreactive character it is. Ask for evidence. Demand facts. Remember its terrible track record.

Because you're the one in charge—not Skippy. And it's about time Skippy remembered that.

The next time anxiety tries to convince you that a minor incident is the end of the world, remember: this is the same voice that once told you the weird noise in your attic was definitely a ghost, and not, as it turned out, a squirrel that had found its way inside. Skippy has no credibility. And it's time we stopped acting like it does.

Chapter 3: Your Brain vs. Reality

Are We Sure My Brain Knows What It's Talking About?

Ladies and Gentlemen, Welcome to the Main Event!

"In this corner, weighing in at approximately three pounds, the undisputed heavyweight champion of overreacting, the sultan of spiral thinking, the monarch of meltdowns, and the emperor of escalation... Your Brain!"

"And in the other corner, coming in with cold, hard facts, rational thinking, and absolutely no tolerance for nonsense, wearing the trunks of truth and the gloves of get-real... it's... Reality!"

This, my friends, is the battle that happens every single day in your head. It's the ultimate showdown, the clash of titans, the epic struggle that makes Marvel movies look like casual disagreements at a book club meeting where everyone secretly picked different books but is too polite to mention it.

And if we're being honest? Your brain is losing. Badly. Like, embarrassingly badly. Like "bringing-a-plastic-spoon-to-a-gunfight" badly. Like "trying-to-empty-the-ocean-with-a-teacup-while-wearing-oven-mitts" badly. Like "using your Netflix password to try to open your front door" badly.

Your brain thinks it's the heavyweight champion, strutting around with its championship belt, while Reality stands in the corner, arms crossed, eyebrows raised, checking its watch, waiting for your brain to notice that its "championship belt" is actually just a fancy paper towel with "WINNER" written on it in crayon. And not even good crayon—we're talking that half-melted one from the bottom of the box that got left in the car during summer.

Meet Your Opponent: Your Brain (A.K.A. The Drama Factory)

Now, let's be clear—your brain means well. It's not trying to sabotage you. It's trying to protect you. It's like an overprotective parent who never quite realized you grew up. It still wants to cut the crusts off your sandwiches and check under the bed for monsters, even though you're 35 and paying a mortgage on a house that you specifically bought because the closets were too small for monsters.

The problem? Your brain has no chill. None. Zero. Zilch. Nada. The concept of "proportional response" is completely foreign to your brain. It's like someone who brings a flamethrower to kill a spider—effective, sure, but maybe just a tiny bit excessive and now your curtains are on fire and the neighbors are calling 911.

Your brain is basically a conspiracy theorist with a podcast. It connects dots that aren't there, finds patterns in random events, and is absolutely convinced that the barista who spelled your name wrong is part of an elaborate plot against you.

It sees one slightly concerning thing and immediately assumes you're in mortal danger. It's the kind of brain that, if left unchecked, will:

- Hear someone laugh across the room and immediately assume it's about you. Because clearly, your slightly mismatched socks are the most hilarious thing anyone has seen all decade, worthy of a Netflix comedy special, and not, you know, the joke someone just told about their cat's Instagram addiction.

- Turn a minor mistake into proof you're a total failure. Because obviously, forgetting one item on your grocery list is the first step in a rapid downward spiral that ends with you living in a cardboard box, sharing half a can of beans with a stray cat named Herbert who judges your life choices even harder than your mother does.

- Convince you that forgetting one email means you'll be fired and living under a bridge by next Tuesday. Your brain has already planned out the exact bridge and is currently decorating your imaginary cardboard home with mental throw pillows and debating whether the "Live, Laugh, Homeless" sign would be too on-the-nose.

- Create an entire alternate universe where that slightly clumsy thing you said to your crush seven years ago has become legendary, told and retold at parties, possibly inscribed on your future tombstone: "Here lies [Your Name]. They once said 'You too' when a server said 'Enjoy your meal,' and society never recovered."

Your brain is so overreactiontic that if it were a person, it would be the one saying, "I can't find my phone! It's gone! I've lost everything! My contacts, my photos, my ENTIRE LIFE IS OVER!" while holding their phone and using the flashlight feature to look for it. That's your brain. That's what you're working with. It's the drama kid from high school who never outgrew the need to make every tiny incident into a five-act Greek tragedy.

Meanwhile, Reality is standing there, arms crossed, waiting patiently, like, "Are you done? Because the phone is literally in your hand, and we have actual problems we could be solving right now, like why you still have 37 unfinished Duolingo lessons and the owl is sending you threatening messages."

Why Your Brain Gets It Wrong So Often

Your brain is running on old, outdated programming. It's like trying to run the latest software on a computer from 1992. It's like trying to play Fortnite on a calculator. It's trying to stream 4K content on dial-up internet. It's working with what it has, but what it has is... not great. It's less "cutting edge technology" and more "rock tied to stick."

Back in the caveman days, it had one job: Keep you alive. It was constantly scanning for tigers, rival tribes, and other dangers that could kill you. And that made sense! When you could be eaten at any moment, a brain that screams "DANGER! DANGER!" at the slightest rustle in the bushes is actually quite useful. That's not anxiety; that's survival.

But now? Now it scans for uncomfortable social interactions and work emails. It's like having a state-of-the-art home security system that goes into full lockdown mode when a leaf blows across your front yard. It's like having a fire alarm that goes off when you light a birthday candle. It's like having a tsunami warning system that activates when you run a bath.

So instead of saying:

"Hey, let's not get eaten by that saber-tooth tiger." (Helpful!)

It now says:

"Hey, that text had a period at the end instead of an exclamation point. That's probably bad. In fact, it's probably a coded message. They probably hate you. They're probably plotting against you right now with their group chat named 'People Who Hate You.' You should spend the next three hours analyzing every interaction you've had with this person over the last six months to figure out exactly when and how you offended them, and then spend another two hours crafting the perfect apologetic-but-not-desperate response, then delete it, then write another one, then accidentally send the draft where you called them a jerk." (Not helpful!)

See the problem?

Your brain is using stone-age survival tactics to deal with modern-day inconveniences. It's like bringing a battle axe to fix your WiFi router. Not only is it the wrong tool for the job, but you're probably going to make things worse, and now you need a new router, and you have to explain to the Geek Squad why your old one has an axe in it.

So when your brain starts freaking out, it's usually wrong. Not just a little wrong. Epically, hilariously, embarrassingly wrong. The kind of wrong that would make great material for a stand-up comedy routine, if it weren't happening inside your head and causing you genuine distress. It's like your brain is delivering the punchline to a joke that isn't funny when you're living it.

The Great Mismatch: Your Brain vs. Modern Life

Let's take a moment to fully appreciate the magnificent absurdity of your brain trying to navigate modern life with its stone-age toolkit. It's like watching your grandpa try to order food using the TV remote.

What Your Brain Was Built For:

- Detecting immediate physical threats

- Making quick fight-or-flight decisions

- Remembering which berries are poisonous

- Recognizing the faces of your tribe members

What Your Brain Is Now Trying to Handle:

- Social media and the constant comparison to others' highlight reels ("Why doesn't MY life look like a perfectly filtered vacation photo?")

- Office politics and passive-aggressive emails ("Per my last email" is modern warfare and you can't convince me otherwise)

- Dating apps and trying to decipher what "Sorry, just saw this!" actually means when they've been active online for three days

- Existential crises about your purpose in life while standing in the cereal aisle trying to decide between 47 different types of breakfast options (Does choosing Captain Crunch over Fiber One say something profound about my character?)

- Trying to figure out if that notification was a like from your crush or just another email from that store where you bought socks once three years ago

It's like asking a calculator to write poetry. It's going to try its best, but the results are going to be... questionable. The emotional equivalent of "Roses are red, violets are 4, error, error, system restore."

Your brain is that friend who still uses a flip phone and suddenly has to navigate a smartphone. It's pressing all the buttons at once, panicking, and somehow ordering 17 pizzas to your ex's address while simultaneously opening 42 browser tabs about conspiracy theories and accidentally setting your Tinder radius to "global" so you're now matching with people in Antarctica.

No wonder it's freaking out. It's doing its best with completely inadequate tools for the job. It's like trying to perform heart surgery with a spork and a glue stick. The intention is good; the execution is... problematic.

Cognitive Distortions: Your Brain's Greatest Hits Album (Of Terrible Remixes)

Anxiety has a whole arsenal of mental tricks that make things seem worse than they really are. These aren't random—they're specific patterns of thought that your brain has perfected over years of practice. It's like your brain has a black belt in making you miserable. It's been training for the Misery Olympics, and it's going for gold.

These are called cognitive distortions, and they are sneaky. They don't announce themselves with a theme song. They don't come with warning labels. They don't introduce themselves like, "Hi, I'm Catastrophizing, and I'll be your cognitive distortion today!" They slide into your consciousness like they belong there, like they're just stating obvious facts instead of serving up premium-grade nonsense with a side of panic.

Let's go over the big ones, the hall-of-famers, the cognitive distortions that deserve their own wing in the "Ways My Brain Lies To Me" museum, complete with interactive exhibits and an overpriced gift shop:

1. Catastrophizing (A.K.A. "Let's Jump Straight to Doom")

What It Is: Your brain's remarkable ability to take a small problem and immediately fast-forward to the absolute worst possible outcome. It's like watching a movie where the opening scene is someone spilling coffee, and the next scene is the apocalypse, with nothing in between to explain how we got there. It's your brain skipping the entire middle of a book and jumping straight from "Once upon a time" to "everyone died tragically ever after."

What It Sounds Like:

- "This small problem is actually a HUGE disaster. In fact, it might be the worst thing that's ever happened to anyone, ever, in the history of humanity. Historians will study this moment. There will be documentaries. 'Where were you when Sarah forgot to attach the file to her email?' people will ask solemnly."

- "I made a mistake. Everything is ruined. My life is over. I should probably just move to a remote mountain cabin and never speak to anyone again. I'll need to learn survival skills. Maybe I should start watching those wilderness shows now to prepare for my new life as a hermit. Do hermits have Wi-Fi? I should look that up."

- "I forgot to respond to that email. My career is over. I'll never work in this town again. I'll have to sell all my possessions and live off the grid. I guess I'll start practicing how to forage for berries and build shelter from pine needles. Will my apartment's security deposit cover the cost of a good tent?"

- "My presentation had a typo. Now everyone knows I'm a fraud. They're probably creating a PowerPoint about my incompetence right now. It will go viral. My name will become synonymous with failure. Children will use 'pulling a [your name]' as slang for completely screwing up. My typo will be added to the dictionary."

How to Talk Back:
- **Zoom Out.** "Okay, theatrics queen brain, let's get some perspective here. Will this matter in a week? A month? A year? When I'm 80 and reflecting on my life, will this even make the highlight reel of memorable moments, or will it be more like that random Tuesday I can't even remember now?"

- **Assign a Realistic Probability.** "On a scale of 1 to 10, how bad is this really? And what are the actual odds that my catastrophic prediction will come true? Am I more likely to experience total ruin, or just momentary discomfort? Is this truly the end of the world, or just an inconvenient Tuesday? If I had to bet my life savings on this disaster actually happening, would I? Or would I keep my money because deep down I know I'm being ridiculous?"

- **Play the Opposite Game.** "Instead of thinking 'This will be terrible,' what about trying something wild—what if it actually goes well? What if this turns out to be no big deal? What if—gasp—something GOOD comes from this? What if instead of ending my career, this mistake actually leads to a solution nobody had thought of? What if I'm not actually destined for a life of cardboard box living?"

- **Track the Path to Doom.** "Okay, brain, walk me through exactly how forgetting to buy milk leads to me living under a bridge. I want a step-by-step breakdown with realistic probabilities at each stage. Show your work. I need a detailed flowchart with citations, please. I'll wait."

2. Mind-Reading (A.K.A. "I Just Know They Hate Me")

What It Is: Your brain's conviction that it knows exactly what other people are thinking, despite the minor inconvenience of not actually being psychic. It's like your brain thinks it has access to everyone else's internal monologue, and surprise! It's always about you, and it's always negative. It's your brain cosplaying as Professor X from X-Men, but instead of using its powers for good, it's just making you feel bad at parties.

What It Sounds Like:
- "They didn't say hi. They must be mad at me. They're probably plotting my social demise as we speak. They've probably started a group chat called 'We Hate

[Your Name]' and they're all in it, even my mom. They're printing t-shirts."

- "They laughed after I spoke—obviously they were making fun of me. They're probably going to tell everyone how ridiculous I am, and I'll be the laughing-stock of the entire office. They've probably already started a TikTok channel dedicated to reenacting everything stupid I've ever said."

- "They haven't texted back yet. I must have done something wrong. They're probably showing my text to other people and laughing. Or maybe they're crafting the perfect message to end our friendship forever. They're probably consulting a team of writers to make sure it's the most devastating rejection possible."

- "My boss wants to meet with me. She's definitely going to fire me. She's probably been collecting evidence of my incompetence for months, building a case against me like a prosecutor preparing for a high-profile trial. She probably has a PowerPoint presentation titled 'Why [Your Name] Is Terrible' with bullet points and animated transitions and everything."

How to Talk Back:
- **Demand Evidence.** "Where's my proof that this is true? Did they actually say they hate me, or am I making assumptions? Can I show beyond a reasonable doubt that my interpretation is correct, or am I running a thought-crime trial with no evidence? Would this hold up in a court of law, or would I be laughed out of Judge Judy's courtroom?"

- **Consider Other Explanations.** "Maybe they were busy trying to remember if they turned off their hair straightener. Maybe they're in a bad mood because they got stuck behind someone paying for groceries with exact change. Maybe they're just bad at texting because they're trying to text while walking their dog who's trying to chase every squirrel in the park. Maybe they have their own anxiety spirals happening about something I said. Maybe—and this is revolutionary—not everything is about me. Maybe they didn't even notice I exist because they're too wrapped up in their own overreactions?"

- **Ask Yourself:** "Would I make this assumption about someone else? If my friend didn't text me back, would I assume they hate me, or would I assume they're busy binge-watching 'The Great British Bake Off'? Why am I holding myself to a different standard? Why am I the main character in everyone else's story?"

- **Remember Your Non-Psychic Status.** "Last I checked, I don't have telepathic powers. I don't have a certificate from the X-Men Academy. I can't actually read minds. So maybe, just maybe, I shouldn't act like my assumptions about other people's thoughts are indisputable facts. Perhaps Professor X I am not."

3. Fortune-Telling (A.K.A. "I Just Know This Will Go Badly")

What It Is: Your brain's unshakeable belief that it can predict the future, despite its long and well-documented history of being completely wrong about things. It's like having a weather forecaster who predicts a category 5 hurricane every single day, regardless of actual conditions. It's your brain with a crystal ball that only shows worst-case scenarios and is probably just a Magic 8-Ball with all the positive answers scratched out.

What It Sounds Like:

- "I'm going to bomb this test. I'll blank out, forget everything I've studied, probably drool on the paper, and the professor will use my test as an example of what not to do for generations of students to come. My test will become a legendary artifact of failure, preserved in a museum of academic disasters."

- "This date will be clumsy and terrible. We'll have nothing to talk about. I'll probably spill something on myself—not just a little drip, but a full entrée, probably something with red sauce that stains permanently. They'll excuse themselves to go to the bathroom and never come back—they might actually climb out the bathroom window to escape me. I'll die alone, surrounded by cats who will eat my face when I'm gone because no one will find my body for weeks."

- "The presentation will be a disaster. I'll forget what I'm saying mid-sentence. Someone will ask a question I can't answer, and then everyone will stand up and point at me in unison, chanting 'Fraud! Fraud!' Everyone will realize I'm a fraud. My career will be over. I might as well update my resume now and start looking into jobs that don't require speaking to humans. Maybe I can be a lighthouse keeper on a remote island with only seagulls for company."

- "I'll never get over this breakup. The pain will be just as intense 40 years from now. I'll be 80 years old, still crying over the relationship that ended when I was 25. My grandchildren will be like, 'Why does Grandma always cry when she hears that song?' and someone will whisper, 'It reminds her of Alex from 2022.' I might as well cancel all future happiness now and invest in tissues and ice cream futures."

How to Talk Back:
- **Challenge the Prediction.** "Have I ever actually predicted the future correctly? What's my track record with these doom prophecies? If I were a professional fortune-teller, would I still have a job with this accuracy rate? Or would I have been run out of town for telling every client they're going to die alone surrounded by half-eaten packages of Oreos?"

- **Recognize the Pattern.** "I've worried before, and things turned out fine. In fact, most of the things I worry about never happen. Maybe, just maybe, this is another false alarm. Maybe my brain is the anxiety equivalent of a car alarm that goes off when a leaf falls on it."

- **Play Out the Best-Case Scenario.** "What if it goes great? What if I ace the test? What if the date is amazing and we end up telling our grandkids about it? What if people love my presentation and I get promoted? Is that outcome actually less likely than my catastrophic prediction, or am I just more comfortable imagining disaster because it feels safer somehow?"

- **Prepare Without Panicking.** "Instead of predicting disaster, what if I put that energy into actual preparation? What concrete steps can I take to improve the situation, rather than just forecasting doom? Could I study instead of spiraling? Practice my presentation instead of predicting its failure? What if preparation is a better use of my mental energy than panicking?"

4. All-or-Nothing Thinking (A.K.A. "Either I'm Amazing or I'm a Failure")

What It Is: Your brain's complete rejection of nuance, middle ground, or shades of gray. It's like having a light switch with only two settings: "I'm a Glorious Success Goddess" and "I'm the Worst Human Who Has Ever Lived." There is no dimmer, no in-between, just blinding light or complete darkness. It's your brain as a melodramatic teenager who says "NOBODY UNDERSTANDS ME" while slamming the door.

What It Sounds Like:

- "I have to be perfect, or I'm worthless. There is no middle ground. Either I am flawless, or I am garbage. These are the only two possibilities. I am either the chosen one or I am nothing. I either win the gold medal or I might as well not have competed at all."

- "If I mess up even a little, I've failed completely. One mistake negates all my previous successes. It's like playing a video game where one wrong move sends you back to level one, erasing all your progress. It's like knocking over the first domino and watching my entire life collapse."

- "If I don't succeed, I might as well not try. Why bother putting in effort if there's any chance of imperfection? Better to avoid the attempt than to risk being anything less than extraordinary. If I can't be the best immediately, I should probably just quit now and save everyone the disappointment."

- "I got feedback on my project. They said it was great overall but suggested two small improvements. Clearly, this means the entire project is a failure, and I should probably resign in disgrace. In fact, I should probably change careers entirely. Perhaps I'm suited to be a hermit living in a cave, where no one can see my inadequacies."

How to Talk Back:

- **Look for the Middle Ground.** "What's a more balanced way to see this? Is there perhaps some vast territory between 'perfect' and 'worthless' where most of human experience actually takes place? Is it possible that life is more like a sliding scale than a binary choice? Can I imagine a world where I'm just... okay?

Not amazing, not terrible, just a regular human doing their best like literally everyone else on the planet?"

- **Recognize Progress.** "Even if I didn't get it 100% right, I still made progress. Partial success is still success. Taking three steps forward and one step back still puts me two steps ahead of where I started. What if I celebrated the improvement instead of mourning the lack of perfection?"

- **Adopt the 80% Rule.** "Good enough is good enough. Perfection is impossible, but excellence is achievable. What if I aimed for 80% instead of 100%? Would the world end? Would anyone even notice the difference? Would the perfection police come and arrest me? Or would life just go on, except I'd be less stressed and actually able to finish things?"

- **Challenge the Binary.** "Life isn't binary. Most things aren't all-or-nothing. They're some-or-more-or-less. Can I find the gray area in this situation instead of defaulting to black-and-white thinking? Can I be a B+ human instead of demanding A+ or nothing? What if I gave myself the same grace I'd give literally anyone else?"

5. Emotional Reasoning (A.K.A. "If I Feel It, It Must Be True")

What It Is: Your brain's insistence that feelings are facts. If you feel anxious, the situation must be dangerous. If you feel inadequate, you must be inadequate. It's like treating your emotions as infallible truth-detectors instead of what they often are: overreactions based on incomplete information. It's your brain turning feelings into CNN Breaking News alerts: "BREAKING: You feel uneasy, therefore EVERYONE is staring at you! More at 11!"

What It Sounds Like:
- "I feel like a failure, therefore I am a failure. My feelings are indisputable evidence of my worth and capability. The Supreme Court of My Mind has ruled, and feelings have been entered into evidence as exhibits A through Z."

- "I feel anxious about this meeting, which proves it's going to go badly. My anxiety is clearly a prophetic warning, not just a chemical reaction in my body.

My nervous system is basically a fortune-telling device, the most accurate oracle since the Oracle at Delphi."

- "I feel like everyone at this party is judging me, so they must be. My discomfort is irrefutable proof of their thoughts. It's not possible that I'm projecting or that I've had three cups of coffee on an empty stomach. No, my feelings are basically mind-reading technology."

- "I don't feel confident about this test, which means I'm not prepared, regardless of how many hours I've studied. My feelings know more about my readiness than my actual study habits. My emotions have a PhD in assessment and evaluation, apparently."

How to Talk Back:
- **Separate Feelings from Facts.** "Just because I feel something doesn't make it true. Feelings are information, not evidence. They're more like weather forecasts than actual weather—predictions, not reality. I can feel like it's going to rain while standing in sunshine."

- **Recognize the Influence.** "My emotions color my perception. When I'm anxious, everything looks threatening. When I'm sad, everything looks hopeless. When I'm hangry, everyone looks annoying. My feelings create filters that distort reality. They're like Instagram filters for my thoughts—they change how things appear without changing what they actually are."

- **Check Your History.** "Have my feelings been reliable predictors in the past? How many times have I felt certain of disaster, only to have things turn out fine? If my feelings were a weather app, would I still use it, or would I have deleted it long ago for being wildly inaccurate?"

- **Ask for Outside Perspective.** "How might someone who doesn't share my current emotional state view this situation? Would they reach the same conclusion? If I described this situation to a friend without mentioning my feelings, what might they say? Would their interpretation match mine, or would they wonder what kind of catastrophizing circus I'm running in my head?"

Step 1: Spot the Lies Your Brain is Telling You

Now that you know your brain is a messy storyteller, like a gossip columnist with zero fact-checkers and a flair for the theatricstic, a tabloid writer who never met a headline they couldn't sensationalize, it's time to start catching it in the act. Think of yourself as an internal detective, investigating the case of "Why Am I Feeling Terrible Right Now?" You're Sherlock Holmes, and your brain is the suspicious character with shifty eyes and a terrible alibi.

When you feel anxious, stop and ask: "What is my brain trying to convince me of right now? What's the story it's selling? What's the headline of this mental tabloid? Is it 'LOCAL PERSON DESTINED FOR HUMILIATION' or 'DISASTER IMMINENT, DETAILS AT 11'?"

Identify the distortion: "Is this catastrophizing? Mind-reading? Fortune-telling? Which cognitive distortion is my brain's flavor of the day? What's today's special in the café of cognitive distortions?"

Challenge it like a detective. "Where's the evidence? What are the facts? What am I assuming that I haven't verified? What holes are in this story? Would this case stand up in court, or would it get thrown out faster than a Bachelor contestant who's 'not here to make friends'?"

Because most of the time? Your thoughts are just thoughts. Not facts. They're just your brain throwing spaghetti at the wall and seeing what sticks. They're rough drafts, not published masterpieces. They're the first pancake in the batch—usually a bit misshapen and not representative of the quality of pancakes to come. They're a first draft written at 3 AM after too much caffeine.

Thoughts happen in your head. Reality happens in the world. And the gap between them is often wide enough to drive a truck through—or maybe a parade of trucks, a marching band, and several elephants, with room to spare.

Step 2: Fact-Check Your Thoughts Like a Journalist

Next time your brain tells you a scary story, fact-check it like you're a hard-hitting investigative journalist who won't publish without multiple sources and concrete evidence. Be the fact-checker your brain desperately needs but doesn't want. Be the editor who sends back the story with "CITATION NEEDED" written in red all over it.

What's the actual evidence? "Is there proof, or is this just a feeling? Do I have concrete, observable facts, or just emotional speculation? Would this evidence hold up in court, or would the judge throw it out as hearsay? Would this pass a peer review, or would academic journals reject it faster than a paper claiming the earth is flat?"

What's a more realistic explanation? "Could there be another reason for this situation? Is there a less catastrophic interpretation that actually makes more sense? If I were writing a balanced news story instead of a sensationalist headline, how would I frame this? What if my first assumption is as accurate as those 'one weird trick' ads on questionable websites?"

What would I tell a friend if they had this thought? "Would I tell them they're doomed, or would I reassure them? Would I agree with their catastrophic interpretation, or would I offer perspective? Why am I treating myself more harshly than I would treat someone I care about? Would I let a friend talk to themselves this way, or would I stage an intervention while shoving ice cream in their face?"

What's my track record with these thoughts? "Have I had similar thoughts before? How did those situations actually turn out? If my anxiety were a weather forecaster, would it still have a job with this accuracy rate? Or would it have been fired after predicting tsunamis in the desert for the fifth time?"

What would someone I respect say about this thought? "What would my mentor/therapist/wisest friend say if I shared this thought with them? Would they validate my catastrophic interpretation, or would they help me see it differently? Would they nod solemnly, or would they try not to laugh while gently pointing out how unlikely my disaster scenario is?"

If your thoughts wouldn't hold up in a court of law, if they wouldn't pass a basic fact-checking process, if they wouldn't make it past an editor's desk, they don't deserve a place in your brain. They've failed the vetting process. They're fake news, and you have every right to label them as such, complete with one of those little warning labels social media puts on questionable content.

Step 3: Name It, Then Reframe It

A powerful way to defuse anxious thoughts? Label them. It's like slapping a giant "FICTION" sticker on a book that's masquerading as your authorized biography. Or like catching your brain running a shady podcast called "Disaster Scenarios with Your Host, Irrational Fear."

"Oh, this is just my brain catastrophizing again. Classic Tuesday afternoon catastrophizing. Nothing to see here, folks. Just my brain's regular programming, right between 'Overthinking Lunch Choices' at 11 and 'Evening Existential Crisis' at 7."

"There's my all-or-nothing thinking kicking in. Right on schedule. Always so punctual with its doom predictions. If being pessimistic were an Olympic sport, my brain would be taking home gold medals like they're participation trophies."

"Ah, mind-reading. My old enemy. Back for another round of 'Let's Pretend We Know What Others Are Thinking: Season 47, Episode 312.' Today's episode: 'Everyone in This Zoom Call Definitely Noticed I Used the Wrong Your/You're in the Chat.'"

By naming the thought, you take away its power—like finding out the terrifying shadow monster on your wall is just your bathrobe hanging on the door. It's no longer your reality—it's just a habit your brain has, like how your uncle insists on forwarding every conspiracy theory email he receives. It's not THE TRUTH; it's just another rerun of "My Brain's Greatest Anxious Hits: Now with Extra Catastrophe!"

This creates distance between you and the thought. You're not your thoughts. You're the person observing your thoughts, like you're sitting in a movie theater watching your brain's amateur film festival of worst-case scenarios. There's a difference between saying "I'm a failure" and "I'm having the thought that I'm a failure." One feels like an inescapable truth carved in stone; the other feels like something you can examine and possibly discard, like that promotional tote bag you got at a conference that you definitely don't need.

Then? Reframe it. Take that distorted thought and reshape it into something more balanced, more realistic, more helpful. Like renovating a house with terrible 1970s decor—the structure might be sound, but those avocado appliances, shag carpets, and wood paneling need a serious update before anyone should have to live there.

Instead of: "I'm going to fail this test." Try "I'll do my best, and that's enough. I've studied, I'm prepared, and regardless of the outcome, this test doesn't define my worth or intelligence any more than my Spotify Wrapped playlist defines my entire personality."

"They hate me." Try "Maybe they're just having a bad day. Or maybe they're dealing with their own anxiety about that weird text they sent at 2 AM last night. Either way, their mood isn't necessarily about me, just like the barista

PART 2: THE GOOD NEWS – YOU CAN REWRITE THE SCRIPT

Now for the good stuff: you don't have to keep listening to that jerk in your head. Your thoughts aren't carved into stone tablets; they're more like something written in dry-erase marker that you've just never bothered to wipe away.

In these next three chapters, we'll dive into exactly how to respond when your brain is being an overreaction queen, the science behind why talking back actually works, and the uncomfortable but necessary art of being kinder to yourself (which, let's be honest, might feel weirder than wearing someone else's shoes at first).

You're about to become the editor-in-chief of your own mental narrative, with full authority to cut unnecessary chapters and rewrite that tired old storyline into something that actually serves you.

Chapter 4: How to Respond When Your Brain is Misbehaving

It's Cute That You Think That, Brain. But No, We're Not Buying Apocalypse Insurance Today.

Your Brain is Overreacting Again. What's Your Move?

Alright, you've made it this far. You now know that your brain is not always your friend. It's more like that one relative who forwards conspiracy theory emails and thinks the government is tracking them through their dental fillings. It's prone to catastrophizing, mind-reading, and making wildly inaccurate predictions about the future. It's like that one friend who watched half of a documentary once and now considers themselves an expert on everything from quantum physics to proper kimchi fermentation techniques.

And yet... when anxiety shows up, we still tend to believe it.

Why?

Because anxiety doesn't just whisper—it kicks the door down wearing a SWAT team outfit, flips the table, and yells, "SOUND THE ALARMS! EVERYTHING IS TERRIBLE! THIS IS NOT A DRILL!" It doesn't politely suggest that maybe things might go wrong; it broadcasts disaster on all frequencies with the confidence of someone announcing the apocalypse on a bullhorn at 5 AM. It's like having your own personal town crier following you around screaming "DOOM! DOOOOOM!" at everything you do. And it's hard to ignore someone screaming about the end of the world, even when you know they've been wrong about it every single time before.

So let's fix that. Let's develop a system for evaluating these overreactiontic proclamations instead of just blindly accepting them like they're breaking news alerts that require your immediate attention.

Today? We fight back. We stop being passive recipients of our brain's nonsense and start being active participants in our own thought processes. We're taking anxiety's megaphone away and replacing it with an application form where it has to actually make its case with evidence. Anxiety now needs to submit its concerns in triplicate, with proper documentation and at least three character references.

The Art of Talking Back to Your Brain

Most people don't talk back to their thoughts. They just... accept them. As if every thought that pops into their head deserves immediate belief and respect, like it's delivering an important telegram from Reality Central. As if their brain is some infallible oracle of truth instead of a chaotic thought generator with zero quality control and questionable motives. It's like taking financial advice from a random person shouting on a street corner.

Imagine if you had a friend (let's call them Disaster Dave or Catastrophe Cathy) who said things like:

"Hey, that small mistake you made? People will remember it forever. They're probably creating a commemorative plaque about it as we speak. There might be a Netflix documentary in production right now: 'The Day Sarah Said The Wrong Thing At The Meeting: A Tragic American Story.'"

"You're going to embarrass yourself. Everyone will judge you. There might even be a formal judging panel with scorecards, like at the Olympics. The Russian judge is particularly harsh."

"You probably have a rare, undiagnosed illness. That minor twinge in your pinky finger? Classic sign of Extremely Rare and Definitely Fatal Pinky Syndrome. I read about it on page 47 of a questionable website once."

Would you just nod along and say, "You're right, Dave. Thanks for your wisdom. I'll start planning my funeral immediately and have started writing farewell letters to everyone I've ever met"?

NO!

You'd say, "That is absolutely ridiculous. What's wrong with you? Have you considered therapy? Or perhaps a hobby that doesn't involve terrorizing your friends with nonsense scenarios? Maybe try knitting or fantasy football instead of catastrophic fortune-telling?"

Well, guess what? Your brain needs that same energy. It needs to be called out on its overreactiontic tendencies, its unfounded claims, its penchant for assuming the worst with zero supporting evidence. It's like a teenager making dramatic predictions about how their life is OVER because they got a B on a quiz.

Let's go over how to talk back when anxiety starts running its mouth. Consider this your comprehensive guide to shutting down your brain's theatrics department – the practical, step-by-step approach to telling anxiety, "That's nice, but we're not doing this today."

Step 1: The "Oh, That's Cute" Method

When your brain presents you with a wildly exaggerated worst-case scenario, try responding with:

"Oh, that's cute. You really went all-in on that one, huh? Did you stay up all night working on that catastrophe, or did it just come to you in a flash of melodramatic inspiration? Should I get you a tiny director's chair and a megaphone for your next disaster production?"

"Wow, 10/10 for creativity, brain. You should write for Netflix. This disaster scenario has better plot twists than most streaming originals. Have you considered a career in dystopian fiction?"

"Oh, we're doing this again? Fascinating. Tell me more about how a minor inconvenience is definitely going to ruin my entire life. I'm on the edge of my seat. Do we get aliens in this version, or are we sticking with the classic 'everyone hates me' storyline?"

"That's adorable. You've really outdone yourself this time. I especially like the part where one clumsy conversation somehow leads to me living alone in the wilderness. Very creative. Gold star for imagination. Maybe we can add some bears and a surprise tornado to really spice up this fantasy?"

"Interesting theory. File that under 'things that would make a great movie but have approximately zero chance of happening in real life.' We could call it 'Anxiety: The Imagining' – coming never to theaters near you."

This is called cognitive defusion. It's a fancy way of saying: When you mock a thought, it loses its power. When you treat an anxious thought like a ridiculous movie plot instead of breaking news, it suddenly seems a lot less compelling. It's like turning the lights on to reveal that the terrifying monster in your room is actually just a pile of laundry on a chair.

Because when you take a step back and see the thought as separate from yourself, it becomes way less scary. It's no longer THE TRUTH; it's just your brain doing that weird thing it does sometimes, like when it gets a random song stuck on repeat for days. It's not you; it's just your brain's latest hit single, "Everything is Terrible (The Remix feat. DJ Catastrophe)."

Here's what happens: By responding with humor or gentle mockery, you:
- Create distance between yourself and the thought

- Reduce the emotional impact of the thought

- Remind yourself that thoughts are just mental events, not facts

- Take back control of the narrative

Try it next time your brain serves up a disaster scenario. Instead of getting pulled into the melodrama, step back, raise an eyebrow, and say, "Nice try, brain. That's hilarious. What else you got? Maybe something with zombies next time to really keep it fresh?" You'll be amazed at how quickly the thought deflates when you refuse to take it seriously.

Step 2: The "Would I Say This to a Friend?" Test

Imagine your best friend comes to you, full of anxiety, and says:
"I feel like I'm a failure. Everyone else is doing better than me. I should probably just give up now and accept my inevitable mediocrity. Maybe I should look into professional hermit opportunities."

"I made a mistake, and now I'm convinced everyone secretly dislikes me. They're probably all in a group chat right now, discussing how much they can't stand me. It's probably called 'Why We Hate Jamie' and has a custom emoji."

"I'm freaking out because I think I might have messed up that email. My entire professional reputation is probably in shambles. Future employers will google me and just find articles about 'The Email Disaster of 2023'."

Would you say:

"Yep. You're right. You're doomed. Let's just assume the worst and give up immediately. In fact, I've already started writing your professional obituary. 'Here lies a career, tragically ended by one uncomfortable email...' I've also taken the liberty of ordering you some sackcloth and ashes for your new failure wardrobe."

OF COURSE NOT.

You'd say:

"Hold on. That's not true. You're being too hard on yourself. Let's take a deep breath and look at the facts. Everyone makes mistakes, and one email isn't going to define your entire professional identity. Also, have you considered that most people are too busy worrying about their own lives to be hyperfocused on your perceived shortcomings? They're probably all at home thinking about what to have for dinner or whether they remembered to switch the laundry to the dryer."

So... why are you so mean to yourself?

We often speak to ourselves in ways we would never speak to someone we care about. We use harsher language, set impossible standards, and offer zero compassion. We become our own worst critics, our own most ruthless judges, our own least supportive friends. We basically become the Regina George of our own mental high school, constantly putting ourselves down with cutting remarks.

The next time your brain starts telling you nonsense, ask:

"Would I say this to a friend? Would I use this tone, this language, this level of catastrophizing? Would I offer this little grace and understanding? Would I tell my best friend they're a complete failure because they forgot one item on their to-do list?"

And if the answer is no, then you should not be saying it to yourself either. You deserve the same kindness, the same perspective, the same benefit of the doubt that you would offer to someone you care about. You wouldn't tell your friend "everyone hates you" because they accidentally sent a text with a typo, so don't tell yourself that either.

Try this exercise: Next time you catch yourself in a negative thought spiral, write down exactly what you're saying to yourself. Then imagine saying those exact words to your best friend, your child, or someone you deeply care about. If you cringe at the thought, if you'd never dream of being so harsh to them, that's a clear sign you need to revise your internal dialogue.

Remember: You're stuck with yourself 24/7. Shouldn't you try to be excellent company? Would you choose to be roommates with someone who constantly criticized everything you did? Then why are you letting your brain be that roommate?

Step 3: The "Let's Get Real" Cross-Examination

Anxiety loves vague, doom-filled statements like:

"This is going to be a disaster." "Everyone thinks I'm annoying." "I'll never get my life together."

CHAPTER 4: HOW TO RESPOND WHEN YOUR BRAIN IS MISBEHAVING

These statements sound convincing because they're broad, absolute, and emotionally charged. They feel true because they play on our insecurities and fears. But they rarely hold up under scrutiny. They're like movie villains who seem terrifying until someone turns on the lights.

That's when you need to interrogate the thought like a skeptical lawyer who's seen it all and isn't buying what the witness is selling. Channel your inner Law & Order character and put that thought on the stand. "Objection, Your Honor! Speculation! Counsel is leading the witness!"

Ask: "Where's the evidence?"

Your brain: "I'm going to fail at this."

*You: "Okay, brain, please present Exhibit A of previous times I've failed in this exact way. I'll need specific examples, dates, and outcomes. Also, please provide statistics on how often I succeed versus how often I fail. Let's see the actual data, not just your feelings on the matter. I'm going to need a spreadsheet, a pie chart, and at least three peer-reviewed studies confirming your position."

Mind-reading anxiety is like assuming everyone is a harsh movie critic reviewing your every move.

You're mind-reading again, assuming everyone noticed your minor mistake as if it's broadcasted on live TV.

Your brain: "Everyone thinks I'm annoying."

*You: "Cool, can you provide a signed document from at least three reliable sources confirming this? Did you conduct a survey? What was your sample size? Was it a representative sample, or just the voices in your head? Also, define 'everyone.' Do you mean literally every human on the planet? Including people in remote villages who have never met me? That seems unlikely. Do babies think I'm annoying? Astronauts? The Queen of England? Everyone is a big claim."

Your brain: "I'm never going to figure my life out."

*You: "Oh? 'Never' is a big word. Are you psychic now? Do you know something I don't? Can you see the future? If so, could you also share next week's lottery numbers? No? Then perhaps we should stick to what we actually know instead of making sweeping predictions about the entirety of my future existence. Let's dial it back to 'I'm feeling uncertain right now' instead of 'My future is eternally doomed.'"

Most anxious thoughts don't hold up under questioning. They're like elaborate houses of cards—impressive at first glance but quick to collapse when you start poking at them. They're all scary facade and no structural integrity.

So cross-examine them until they break down like a bad witness on the stand. Ask for specifics. Demand evidence. Challenge absolutist language like "always," "never," and "everyone." Look for patterns of exaggeration and catastrophizing. Turn your anxiety from an authoritative expert into a nervous witness who can't keep their story straight.

And remember, the burden of proof lies with the anxious thought. It needs to prove its case beyond a reasonable doubt—not the other way around. You don't need to prove it's false; it needs to prove it's true. And spoiler alert: it usually can't. It's usually making claims that would get thrown out of any reasonable courtroom for lack of evidence.

Step 4: The "Name It, Then Reframe It" Strategy

One of the most powerful things you can do when an anxious thought shows up?
Name it.

There's something almost magical about identifying and labeling a thought pattern. It's like turning on the lights in a dark room—what seemed scary and overwhelming suddenly becomes recognizable and manageable. It's like finally figuring out what that weird noise in your car is—still annoying, but no longer mysteriously terrifying.

When you say,

"Oh, there's my catastrophizing again. Right on schedule. Always so punctual with the doom predictions. Never misses an appointment to tell me everything is falling apart."

"Ah, my brain is fortune-telling. Classic. Reading the tea leaves of disaster without any actual evidence. Breaking out the crystal ball of doom for another psychic prediction that will probably never come true."

"This is just my social anxiety being theatricstic. It loves to assume everyone notices and remembers my every move, like I'm the star of a reality show that only exists in my head. 'Keeping Up With My Embarrassing Moments' – now in its 35th season."

You take away its power. You strip it of its disguise as an indisputable fact and reveal it for what it truly is: just a thought pattern, a habit, a familiar but unreliable narrator in the story of your life. It's like catching the Wizard of Oz behind the curtain—suddenly not so intimidating after all.

Because now, it's just a habit—NOT reality. It's not THE TRUTH descending from on high; it's just your brain running one of its familiar programs, like an old computer that keeps trying to open a software program you uninstalled years ago. It's your mental Windows Vista trying to run even though you've upgraded several times since.

Then, reframe it. Take that distorted thought and reshape it into something more balanced, more accurate, more helpful. Like a potter working with clay, you can take the raw material of your thought and mold it into a more useful form. Or like editing a really theatricstic first draft into something more reasonable.

Instead of:

"I'm going to bomb this presentation." to Try: "I might feel nervous, but I'm prepared. Even if it's not perfect, it doesn't have to be. I've practiced, I know my material, and one presentation doesn't define my entire career. Plus, remember that time I thought I would bomb the Johnson pitch and ended up getting a standing ovation? My anxiety has a terrible track record as a predictor."

"That person didn't text back, they must hate me." to Try: "They're probably just busy scrolling through TikTok or trying to decide what to watch on Netflix. People have lives that don't revolve around their phones. Or maybe they're dealing with their own anxiety about what to say. Either way, it's likely not about me. Remember how I didn't text Mom back for three days last week because I got distracted by that documentary about penguins? People get distracted."

"Everything is falling apart." to Try: "This is a challenge, but I can handle it. I've faced difficult situations before and made it through. This specific issue is manageable, even if it feels overwhelming right now. Remember when my car broke down in the middle of nowhere and I still managed to get home? That felt like the end of the world too, but I figured it out."

"I'll never be good enough." to Try: "I'm a work in progress, just like everyone else. 'Good enough' is a moving target, and I'm doing my best with the resources I have right now. Even Beyoncé has bad days, and she's Beyoncé."

"Everyone at this party is judging me." to Try: "Most people are too focused on themselves to be meticulously judging others. They're worrying about their own outfit choices and whether they have food in their teeth. And even if someone does judge me, that says more about them than it does about me. Plus, I'm wearing this amazing shirt that deserves to be noticed."

Your thoughts aren't the boss of you. You get to decide which ones you believe. You are allowed to edit, revise, and rewrite the narrative your brain presents to you, like a strict editor who sends back a writer's first draft with "needs work" written in red pen.

This isn't about toxic positivity or pretending everything is great when it isn't. It's about accuracy—replacing distorted, exaggerated thoughts with more balanced, realistic ones. It's not "think happy thoughts"; it's "think accurate thoughts." It's like adjusting a funhouse mirror so it shows your actual reflection instead of a warped version.

Step 5: Play Out the Absolute Worst-Case Scenario (And Laugh at It)

Anxiety loves vague, ominous threats. It thrives on that foggy sense of impending doom without specifics. It's like a horror movie that keeps the monster in the shadows—as soon as you turn on the lights and get a good look, it's usually way less scary than you imagined. Often it's just a coat rack with a hat on it that looked terrifying in the dark.

So let's say your brain is panicking over a small mistake at work.

Your brain: "Oh no, I messed up that report. This is it. My boss will fire me. I'll be unemployed. I'll lose everything. I'll have to move into a van down by the river. I'll have to learn to fish for my dinner. My future grandchildren will tell stories about how I destroyed the family legacy with one spreadsheet error. They'll write folk songs about my downfall."

You: "Okay, let's actually walk through this ridiculous scenario. Let's follow this to its 'logical' conclusion. Let's ride this anxiety rollercoaster all the way to the end and see where we land."

Step 1: You get fired (unlikely, as most companies don't terminate employees over a single mistake unless it's catastrophic, which this wasn't). But let's say they do – they call you in and overreactiontically point to the door while everyone watches in shocked silence.

Step 2: You apply for another job (plenty of those exist, and you have skills and experience that didn't magically disappear because of one error). You update your LinkedIn profile and suddenly remember you actually hated that job anyway.

Step 3: You get hired somewhere else (because that's how employment works, and there's actually a rather robust job market for people who aren't perfect but are generally competent). Your new boss doesn't start the interview with "Tell me about that time you messed up a spreadsheet at your last job."

Step 4: You DO NOT end up homeless because you made one typo on a spreadsheet. That's not how homelessness works. That's not how anything works. There is no direct pipeline from "Excel error" to "cardboard box residence."

See how dumb that sounds? When you actually walk through the steps of your anxiety's "inevitable" outcome, it starts to fall apart. The logical leaps become apparent. The exaggerations become ridiculous. The worst-case scenario, when examined closely, is either highly unlikely or not actually that catastrophic.

This is called "de-catastrophizing." It forces your brain to realize that even the worst-case scenario is usually NOT that bad. And more importantly, it's usually manageable. You have resources, skills, support systems, and experience that would help you handle even a genuinely bad outcome. You've survived 100% of your worst days so far, which is a pretty good track record.

And 99.9% of the time? It never happens anyway. Your brain is like a weather forecaster who predicts a category 5 hurricane every single day, even in the desert. After the 300th false alarm, maybe it's time to stop evacuating and just bring an umbrella instead. Maybe it's time to recognize that your anxiety's weather reports are about as reliable as a chocolate teapot.

Try this exercise: Next time you're anxious about something, ask yourself these questions:

- What's the absolute worst thing that could happen? (Be specific—no vague doom allowed. "Everything will fall apart" is not specific. "I might get a C on this paper" is specific.)

- How likely is that worst-case scenario? (Be honest—assign an actual percentage. And remember that "50/50" usually means "I have no idea" not "this is an actual coin flip.")

- If it did happen, could I cope with it? (What resources, skills, or support would help? Who could you call? What steps could you take?)

- What's a more realistic outcome based on past experience? (How have similar situations turned out before? What's your actual track record with these kinds of situations?)

More often than not, you'll find that the worst-case scenario is both unlikely and survivable. And knowing that can take a lot of the power out of anxiety's threats. It's like realizing the "monster" under your bed is just a dust bunny with attitude.

Step 6: Remember That You've Survived 100% of Your Worst Days So Far

Here's something anxiety conveniently forgets: your track record for surviving difficult days is impeccable. You've made it through every single bad day, every embarrassing moment, every failure, every heartbreak, every disappointment that you've ever experienced. Your survival rate thus far is 100%. You are literally undefeated against bad days.

That's not just positive thinking; that's a statistical fact.

So when your brain is telling you that you can't handle something, remind it:

"Actually, I have quite an impressive résumé of surviving difficult situations. Remember that time I thought I couldn't handle [challenging past experience], but I did? Or that time [embarrassing thing] happened, and I was certain my life was over, but somehow I'm still here and it's now just a funny story I tell at parties? I've navigated countless situations that my anxiety told me would be unbearable, and yet, here I stand, still going strong and occasionally even thriving."

This isn't about minimizing genuine challenges or suggesting that difficult experiences don't hurt. They do. But remembering your own resilience—your demonstrated capacity to weather storms and keep going—can be a powerful antidote to anxiety's claim that you won't be able to cope with what's ahead.

Your brain might be a theatrics queen, but you? You're a survivor. And that's not just a nice sentiment; it's a fact backed up by your entire life history so far. You've survived embarrassing moments, bad haircuts, fashion choices from 2003, breakups, job interviews, public speaking, and countless other things your anxiety swore would destroy you.

Your Thoughts Are Not The Boss of You

Your brain is going to keep throwing overreactiontic nonsense at you. That's its job. That's what brains do. They generate thoughts—thousands of them, every day. Some useful, some ridiculous, some downright preposterous, and some that make you wonder if you accidentally ingested something hallucinogenic.

Your job?

Talk back.

Your thoughts are just suggestions, not facts. They're like unsolicited advice from strangers on the internet—sometimes helpful, often misguided, occasionally bizarre, and always optional to follow. They're like those weird product recommendations that pop up when you're online shopping – sometimes oddly specific, rarely what you actually need.

You don't have to listen. You don't have to believe everything you think. You are allowed to challenge, question, and rewrite the thoughts that hold you back.

Think of it this way: Your brain is like a very enthusiastic but not particularly accurate news channel that's constantly broadcasting headlines. You get to be the discerning viewer who says, "I'm going to fact-check that before I believe it." You get to change the channel when the programming isn't serving you. You get to turn down the volume when it's getting too loud. You get to say "I'm not watching 'Disaster Theater' today, I think I'll switch to something more uplifting."

Because at the end of the day?

You are in charge. Not your brain. Not your anxiety. Not the melodramatic fortune-teller living in your head. You.

And the more you practice talking back—challenging, questioning, reframing—the better you get at it. It becomes a habit, a skill, a superpower. Your anxiety doesn't disappear (sorry, that's not how brains work), but it stops running the show. It becomes background noise instead of the main event. It becomes that weird street performer you walk past on your way to more important things, not the director of your life story.

And that, my friend, is how you start taking back control of your mind.

Chapter 5: The Science of Talking Back to Yourself

No, Brain. We're Not Doing This Today. I've Seen Your TripAdvisor Reviews and They're Terrible.

So, Talking Back to Your Brain Actually Works?

Yes. Yes, it does.

And not in some woo-woo, "just think happy thoughts and sprinkle yourself with magical confidence dust" way. This isn't about ignoring your anxiety or pretending everything is fine when it's clearly not. This isn't about positive affirmations that you don't believe or visualizing success while your brain screams about impending doom in the background like a tornado siren that won't shut off.

This is about training your brain—the same way you train a hyperactive dog that barks at literally everything including its own shadow, the refrigerator humming, and the concept of Tuesdays. You don't just hope the dog will magically stop barking one day. You don't put on noise-canceling headphones and pretend the barking isn't happening while your neighbors file noise complaints. You implement specific techniques to change the behavior.

Right now, your brain is reactive. It panics first, questions later (if ever). It jumps to conclusions, assumes the worst, and delivers catastrophes with the speed and efficiency of Amazon Prime. One-click ordering for disaster scenarios, delivered straight to your consciousness before you've even had your morning coffee. "Thanks for subscribing to Disaster Prime! Your package of irrational fears will arrive in the next 30 seconds!"

But with the right strategies? You can rewire it. You can train it to pause, evaluate, and respond instead of just reacting. You can teach it to question before catastrophizing. You can help it develop the mental equivalent of impulse control. You can essentially install a spam filter for your thoughts so the "YOU'VE WON A FREE ANXIETY ATTACK" emails go straight to trash.

So today, we're breaking down the science of why talking back to your brain actually works—and how to train your mind to be less of a disaster factory. No magic, no wishful thinking, just practical neuroscience and psychological techniques that have actual evidence behind them. Think of it as sending your brain back to school, except this time it's going to learn something useful instead of that weird fact about mitochondria being the powerhouse of the cell.

Neuroplasticity: Your Brain is Moldable (Like Play-Doh, But More Complicated and Less Tasty)

Here's some great news:

Your brain is not a fixed, unchangeable lump of neurons. It's flexible. It's adaptable. It's constantly rewiring itself based on what you do repeatedly. Your brain can change—not just in childhood, but throughout your entire life. It's not set in concrete; it's more like a Lego construction that can be rebuilt and reconfigured well into your 90s.

This concept is called neuroplasticity—which is a fancy way of saying:

The thoughts you focus on the most get stronger. The thoughts you ignore get weaker. Your brain literally rewires itself based on what you practice.

Think of it like a path in a forest. The more you walk a particular route, the clearer and more well-established that path becomes. Meanwhile, the paths you don't use start to grow over with weeds and eventually disappear back into the forest. It's like those desire paths you see cutting across grassy areas on college campuses—they start as just a few footprints, but with enough traffic, they become the main route that everyone uses.

So right now? If your brain is really good at overthinking, panicking, and assuming the worst...

That's because it has practiced doing that for years. You've worn a deep, clear path to Catastrophe Town, and your brain can find its way there with its eyes closed, in the dark, during a storm. You're an expert at anxiety because you've put in the hours. You've earned your black belt in worst-case scenarios. You've got a PhD in Panic, a Master's in Mayhem, and a Bachelor's in Bad Outcomes. You're essentially the LeBron James of negative thinking—you've achieved greatness through practice.

But guess what? If you start practicing challenging those thoughts, questioning them, and replacing them with better ones—your brain rewires itself to do THAT instead. You can create new pathways, new neural connections, new habits of thought that lead to more accurate, more helpful interpretations of reality. It's like building a fancy new highway that bypasses Anxiety City completely and leads straight to Rational Response Resort, where the weather is mild and the panic attacks are minimal.

It's not magic. It's neuroscience. It's the way your brain is designed to work. It's your brain's superpower—the ability to reorganize itself by forming new neural connections throughout your life.

And this is why talking back to your brain isn't just fun—it's necessary. It's how you build those new pathways. It's how you create alternative routes that don't all lead to panic and despair. It's how you give your future self more options when faced with uncertainty. It's like being both the city planner and construction crew for your mind, designing and building better mental infrastructure.

This also means that changing your thought patterns takes time. You didn't develop your anxiety overnight, and you won't rewire your brain overnight either. But with consistent practice, you can create significant, lasting change in how your brain processes information and responds to potential threats. Rome wasn't built in a day, and neither is a calmer, more rational thought process—but both are absolutely achievable with persistence.

Step 1: Catch It, Challenge It, Change It

(A.K.A. The Three C's of Rewiring Your Anxious Brain, or "How to Stop Your Brain from Auditioning for a Disaster Movie")

Every time anxiety shows up, you now have a three-step process:
1. **CATCH IT** (Notice the thought for what it is, like catching your dog eating your shoes before he swallows the whole thing.)

Your brain: "This is going to be a disaster. Everything will fall apart. The presentation will bomb, your career will end, and you'll have to sell hand-knitted scarves on Etsy to survive."

Mind-reading anxiety is like assuming everyone is a harsh movie critic reviewing your every move.

You: "Oh hey, there's my anxiety doing its thing again. I see you there, brain, with your disaster movie script. That's a fascinating catastrophe you've crafted."

Catching means developing awareness of your thought patterns. It means noticing when anxiety shows up and identifying the specific thought that's causing distress. This step alone is powerful because it interrupts the automatic process of accepting the anxious thought as truth. It's like hitting the pause button right when the horror movie starts, before you get too scared.

Think of it like setting up a mental checkpoint. Before any thought gets to proceed into "Absolute Truth" territory, it has to go through inspection. "Excuse me, thought, I'm going to need to see some ID and search your luggage before you go any further. Is that a concealed catastrophe you're carrying?"

1. **CHALLENGE IT** (Ask if it's actually true, or just anxiety wearing a convincing costume.)

You: "Okay, but do I have real evidence for this, or am I just assuming? Is this fact or opinion? What's my track record with these kinds of predictions? Haven't I predicted 37 career-ending disasters in the past year, and I still have the same job? Is there another way to interpret this situation that doesn't involve living in my parents' basement at age 45?"

Challenging means examining the thought critically instead of accepting it at face value. It means questioning its accuracy, its helpfulness, and its origins. It's about becoming an investigative journalist of your own mind, fact-checking before publishing anything to your internal newsfeed. It's like being the Sherlock Holmes of your own thoughts—"Elementary, my dear brain. Your theory has several fatal flaws."

This step is crucial because most anxious thoughts don't hold up well under scrutiny. They're like elaborate conspiracy theories—they seem compelling at first glance but fall apart when you start asking for concrete evidence. They're like those clickbait headlines that promise "You Won't BELIEVE What Happened Next!" but the actual article is three boring paragraphs about nothing.

1. **CHANGE IT** (Replace it with something more accurate and helpful, like swapping out a horror movie for a less terrifying documentary.)

You: "This might be uncomfortable, but I can handle it. I've dealt with difficult situations before, like that time the projector failed and I had to give the entire presentation from memory. Even if it doesn't go perfectly, it won't be the end of the world. In fact, most people will probably be checking their emails during my presentation anyway, so they might not even notice if I stumble over a few words."

Changing means actively creating an alternative thought that's both more accurate and more helpful. Not a sugar-coated fantasy, but a realistic perspective that acknowledges challenges without catastrophizing them. It's about giving your brain a better script to work with. It's like being the editor of your thought process, cutting out the unnecessary melodrama while keeping the useful information.

This isn't about being blindly optimistic. It's about being balanced and fair in your assessments. It's replacing "This will be a complete disaster, everyone will laugh, and I'll be fired on the spot" not with "This will be amazing and they'll carry me around the office on their shoulders!" but with "This might be challenging, but I have resources to cope with it, and most presentations at work are just average anyway."

If you do this over and over again, your brain starts learning. It starts to internalize this new process. The mental checkpoint becomes more automatic. The questioning becomes more habitual. The reframing becomes more natural. It's like training for a marathon—the first mile is awful, but it gets easier the more you practice.

At first, it might feel fake. Your brain won't believe you. The new thoughts will feel forced and artificial, like you're just going through the motions. Your emotional state might not change immediately. Your brain will be like a suspicious teenager: "Whatever, you're just saying that."

But after enough repetitions?

Your new thoughts become automatic. They start to feel natural. The pathway becomes established. The neural connections strengthen. The habit forms. It's like learning to drive—at first, you have to think about every single action, but eventually, you can do it while singing along to the radio.

And suddenly, instead of thinking, "Oh no, I'm doomed"—your brain starts thinking, "Okay, this isn't ideal, but I've handled worse, like that time I accidentally sent that email to the entire company instead of just Jim." Not because you're forcing it to, but because that's now the path of least resistance. That's the route your brain naturally takes, because you've walked it so many times deliberately.

That's rewiring. That's neuroplasticity in action. That's your brain adapting to the training you've been providing. That's your brain muscles getting stronger in exactly the areas you've been exercising.

CHAPTER 5: THE SCIENCE OF TALKING BACK TO YOURSELF   65

Step 2: Your Brain is a Google Search—Change What You Type (And Stop Googling "Worst-Case Scenarios" at 3 AM)

Here's something wild:

Your brain works a lot like Google.

Whatever you search for? It will find. Your brain is an expert at confirming what you ask it to confirm. It's a search engine designed to retrieve information that matches your query, with algorithms heavily biased toward finding what you're looking for. It's like if you search for "evidence that aliens built the pyramids"—Google will find you that content, not because it's necessarily true, but because that's what you asked for.

Let me compile them chronologically, starting with that time in second grade when you enthusiastically waved back at someone only to realize they were waving at the person behind you. I've been saving these in a special file labeled 'SOCIAL DISASTERS' for just such an occasion. I've got video footage, surround sound, and detailed commentary from imaginary critics who were there.

If you search for: "What if everything goes wrong?"

Your brain will say: "Great question! Let's imagine ALL the possible disasters in detail. I've prepared a comprehensive PowerPoint presentation with 74 slides of worst-case scenarios, complete with realistic sound effects and emotional simulations. Would you like the extended director's cut version with bonus catastrophes not seen in theaters?"

BUT...

If you search for: "What's something I handled well before?"

Your brain will say: "Oh! Here's a list of things you've been strong through. Remember that time you thought you couldn't handle that big presentation, but you did it anyway and it turned out fine? Or when you were sure that difficult conversation would be a disaster, but you navigated it successfully? I have records of those too, they're just usually filed under 'BORING NORMAL OUTCOMES' so I don't bring them up as often because they lack overreactiontic tension."

If you search for: "How can I make this situation work?"

Your brain will say: "Let's come up with solutions instead of panic. We could try approach A, or perhaps method B. Maybe we could ask for help with aspect C. There are actually several avenues we could explore here that don't involve declaring emotional bankruptcy and moving to a remote cabin in the woods."

You get to control the search terms. This is a profoundly important realization. You're not just a passive receiver of your brain's output—you actively influence what it produces by how you frame your internal questions. You're essentially programming your own search algorithm.

Change what you ask, and your brain will find different answers. This isn't magical thinking; it's directing your attention and cognitive resources toward different types of information. It's using the search algorithm to your advantage instead of letting it run wild with unhelpful queries. It's being a smart Google user of your own brain.

Try this experiment: For one full day, notice the implicit questions in your thoughts. Are you constantly asking yourself "What's wrong with me?" or "Why does this always happen to me?" or "What will go wrong next?" Those are search terms, and your brain is diligently returning results like the world's most conscientious but slightly unhinged personal assistant.

Then practice deliberately changing those questions. Instead of "What will go wrong?" try "What might go right?" Instead of "Why am I so bad at this?" try "What have I learned from doing this before?" Instead of "Why is everyone else better at life than me?" try "What's one thing I'm handling well right now?" It's like switching from searching "terminal illnesses that start with headaches" to "effective headache remedies."

You'll be amazed at how different the search results can be when you change the query. You'll get completely different data from your brain's database just by asking better questions.

Step 3: Turn Anxiety Into an Argument That You Win (Because Anxiety is Like That Friend Who Always Has to Be Right)

Your anxiety wants to argue with you. It's like that person on the internet who's always looking for a fight, posting inflammatory comments and waiting for someone to take the bait. It's that guy in the comments section who types in ALL CAPS and ends everything with "WAKE UP SHEEPLE!!!"

Fine. LET'S ARGUE. But we're going to do it on your terms, not anxiety's. We're going to make it a structured debate where evidence matters and logical fallacies get called out. We're going to use Robert's Rules of Order while anxiety is trying to use playground taunts.

Here's how this works:

Step 1: Write down the anxious thought.

Example: "What if I fail this project and ruin my entire career and end up living in a cardboard box under a bridge where all my former colleagues will walk by and say 'there's that person who failed that one project'?"

Get it out of your head and onto paper (or screen). This alone creates some distance—now it's a statement to be examined, not just an experience you're having. It's like capturing that internet troll's comment so you can dissect it properly instead of just reacting emotionally. It's like taking a screenshot of the ridiculous text your ex sent so you can show it to your friends for a proper analysis.

Step 2: Pretend your best friend just said this. How would you respond?

Would you say, "Yep. You're a disaster. Just give up now. I've already called the bridge authority to reserve you a prime spot under the north side. Would you prefer cardboard or plastic for your new home?"?

NO. You'd say, "Okay, calm down. That's a little extreme, don't you think? You'll be fine. One project doesn't define your entire career. Even if it doesn't go perfectly, you'll learn from it and move forward. Remember when you thought that last project would be a disaster, and it turned out fine? Remember when you were convinced you'd bomb that presentation but ended up getting compliments? Your disaster predictions have about the same accuracy rate as a weather forecaster in Seattle saying 'definitely no rain tomorrow.'"

This step leverages something psychologists call the "Solomon Effect"—the phenomenon where we're often better at solving other people's problems than our own. We can be remarkably wise and compassionate when it comes to others, while being harsh and catastrophic with ourselves. This technique harnesses that external perspective for your own benefit. It's like consulting a wiser version of yourself who doesn't have emotional skin in the game.

Step 3: Write down your response.

Something like:

"Even if I mess up, it's not the end of the world. I've succeeded before, and I can fix mistakes. I am not my worst moment. My career is built on many projects and interactions, not just this one. Plus, I'm preparing and doing my best, which significantly reduces the chances of catastrophic failure. And let's be real, in five years, no one will even remember this project—they'll be too busy worrying about their own stuff. Worst case scenario, I can always add 'Expert Bridge Dweller' to my LinkedIn skills."

Put that rational, compassionate response in writing. Make it concrete. Be as thorough and persuasive as you would be if you were really trying to help someone you care about see things more clearly. Don't hold back—bring your A-game rebuttal.

Your brain loves patterns. So if you keep practicing this every time anxiety shows up, your brain will start doing it automatically. The internal argument becomes less melodramatic, less one-sided, more balanced. You start automatically considering multiple perspectives instead of just accepting anxiety's prosecutor-style opening statement as the final verdict. It's like training your inner defense attorney to automatically object when anxiety starts presenting inadmissible evidence.

This is cognitive restructuring in action—systematically identifying distorted thoughts and replacing them with more balanced ones. It's not about shutting down the anxious voice entirely; it's about making sure the rational voice gets equal time in the conversation. It's making sure both sides of your brain's debate team are equally prepared.

Step 4: Use the "Would I Bet Money on That?" Trick

This is one of my favorite tricks. It cuts through emotional reasoning better than almost anything else I've found. It brings the cold, hard reality of financial risk into your emotional thought process.

When anxiety tells you something terrible will happen, ask yourself:

"Would I bet $100 that this is true?"

Or take it further: "Would I bet my life savings on this prediction? Would I be willing to go into debt if I'm wrong? Would I put my next mortgage payment on this outcome in Vegas?"

Because guess what?

99% of the time, you wouldn't.

Because deep down, you know your anxious thoughts aren't always accurate.

Your brain just loves to assume the worst.

There's a huge difference between feeling like something is true and being willing to put actual resources on the line to back up that belief. This question forces you to distinguish between the two. It's like the difference between saying "I think that restaurant is terrible" and actually investing your life savings to short their stock.

So when your brain says:

"They secretly hate me. They're going to create an anti-fan club with t-shirts and meetings."

"This will be a disaster. Cities will fall. History books will mention this presentation in the chapter on tragic failures."

"I'm definitely going to fail. It's as certain as gravity."

Ask yourself:

"Would I bet money on this? Would I stake something valuable on the accuracy of this prediction? If this were a gambling scenario, would I put my chips on this outcome? Would I call my financial advisor and tell them to invest based on this prediction? If a bookie offered me odds on this outcome, would I take them?"

If not? Then why are you believing it? Why are you willing to bet your peace of mind, your emotional wellbeing, your mental energy on a prediction you wouldn't back financially? If you wouldn't risk $20 on it, why are you risking your entire mental health?

This question helps reveal the difference between anxious certainty ("This will definitely be a disaster!") and actual confidence based on evidence. It exposes how little faith we actually have in our catastrophic predictions, even as we're being tormented by them. It shows the gap between what we fear and what we actually think is likely.

It's a powerful reality check that can quickly cut through the fog of anxiety and bring clarity to your thought process. It's like turning on the house lights in the middle of a horror movie—suddenly things aren't so scary anymore.

Step 5: The Power of "And" Statements (Because Life is Not Black and White; It's More Like a Jackson Pollock Painting)

Anxiety loves absolutes. It thrives on black-and-white thinking, on rigid either/or dichotomies, on extreme conclusions. It wants everything to be all-or-nothing, success-or-failure, perfect-or-worthless. It's like a toddler who only knows "yes" and "no" with no concept of "maybe" or "sometimes."

It tells you:

"I'm nervous, so I can't do this. Nervousness completely disables all my abilities."

"I made a mistake, so I'm a failure. One error nullifies every achievement I've ever had."

"I feel uncomfortable, so something is wrong. Discomfort is always an emergency warning signal."

"I don't know exactly what will happen, so it will probably be bad. Uncertainty always leads to disaster."

These are all statements that draw absolute conclusions from partial information. They take one element of reality and extrapolate wildly from it, ignoring all nuance and complexity. They're like saying "It's raining today, therefore summer is canceled."

But real life? Real life is full of AND statements. Real life is messy, contradictory, and full of seemingly opposing truths existing side by side. Real life happens in the gray areas between extremes. Real life is both/and, not either/or. Real life is complicated, like a TV series with multiple seasons, not a black and white silent film.

Try these instead:

"I'm nervous, AND I can still do this. My nervousness doesn't eliminate my capabilities. In fact, the adrenaline might actually help me be more alert and focused."

"I made a mistake, AND I'm still capable. This error doesn't define me or nullify my skills. It's just one data point in a vast collection of experiences that make up my life."

"I don't feel great today, AND I can still make progress. My feelings aren't an accurate measure of my capacity. I can feel terrible and still accomplish things, just like I've done many times before."

"This is challenging, AND I'm up for the challenge. Difficulty doesn't mean impossibility. In fact, the things that challenge me are often the most rewarding in the end."

"I'm uncertain about the outcome, AND I can handle whatever happens. Not knowing doesn't mean it will be bad. Sometimes the best things in life come from situations I couldn't predict."

One word—"AND"—turns an anxious statement into a balanced one. It acknowledges the first reality without letting it dictate an extreme conclusion. It creates space for complexity, for nuance, for the both/and nature of human experience. It's like upgrading from a flip phone that can only do one thing at a time to a smartphone that can run multiple apps simultaneously.

This simple linguistic shift can have profound effects on your thought patterns. It's a small tool that helps break the spell of all-or-nothing thinking that feeds so much of our anxiety. It's like adding a new color to a painting that was previously just black and white.

Practice adding "AND" to your anxious thoughts. See how it immediately opens up possibilities beyond the either/or trap that anxiety set for you. Notice how it creates breathing room, options, alternate interpretations that anxiety tried to exclude. It's like having a key that unlocks doors you didn't even know existed.

Step 6: Develop an Evidence-Based Reputation System (Because Your Anxiety is Like a Weatherman Who Always Predicts Hurricanes)

Your anxious brain has a terrible track record as a predictor, but it never seems to realize this. It continues making catastrophic forecasts with absolute confidence, never acknowledging how often it's been wrong before. It's like that friend who confidently gives you stock tips but somehow never mentions all the times their picks tanked.

It's time to start keeping score.

Create an actual log of your brain's predictions versus outcomes. Every time your anxiety makes a specific prediction ("This presentation will be a disaster," "They won't like me," "I'll definitely fail this test"), write it down. Then, after the event occurs, write down what actually happened. It's like being the fact-checker for your anxiety's wild claims.

Over time, you'll compile a database of evidence about how accurate your anxious predictions really are. And spoiler alert: they're usually way off base. Like, not even in the same galaxy as reality.

This serves several purposes:

It holds your anxiety accountable for its predictions, like forcing a politician to answer for their campaign promises It creates a reality check you can reference when future anxious thoughts arise, like having a cheat sheet during a test It builds a case for why you shouldn't automatically believe every anxious forecast, like developing an immunity to spam emails It gives you concrete evidence of your resilience and ability to handle situations, like a highlight reel of your greatest hits

Think of it as developing a reputation system for your thoughts. If a certain type of thought has been wrong 90% of the time in the past, why would you give it the benefit of the doubt now? If your catastrophic predictions have a 5% accuracy rate, they should be treated with the appropriate level of skepticism. You wouldn't keep buying products from a company that sent you the wrong items 95% of the time, so why keep buying what your anxiety is selling?

This evidence-based approach helps move you from emotional reasoning ("I feel like this will be a disaster, so it must be true") to rational assessment ("My anxiety has predicted disasters many times before, and they rarely materialize"). It's like developing a sophisticated BS detector for your own thoughts.

You Can Rewire Your Brain (Yes, YOU, Even If You've Been Anxiously Overthinking Since Childhood)

Right now, your brain is probably really good at worrying.

Why? Because it has practiced worrying for YEARS.

But guess what?

If you practice questioning your thoughts, your brain will learn to do that instead.

If you practice replacing anxious thoughts, your brain will get better at it.

If you practice talking back, your brain will stop assuming everything is a disaster.

This is science. This is how your brain works. This is neuroplasticity in action, and it's available to every human being with a functioning brain—not just the naturally calm ones, not just the mindfulness experts, not just the people who seem to have it all together. It's as available to you as it is to anyone else.

It's available to you, right now, regardless of how long you've struggled with anxiety. Your brain can change. Your thought patterns can shift. Your automatic responses can be rewired. You're not stuck with the mental software you're currently running.

Will it happen overnight? No. That would be like expecting to get six-pack abs after one sit-up. Will it require consistent practice? Yes. Will there be setbacks along the way? Absolutely. There will be days when your anxiety seems to be winning, when your brain reverts to its old patterns, when talking back feels impossible.

But with each repetition, each time you catch, challenge, and change an anxious thought, you're building new neural pathways. You're creating alternatives to the well-worn anxiety routes in your brain. You're establishing new habits that will eventually become as automatic as the old ones. It's like learning to type—at first you hunt and peck, but eventually your fingers know where to go without conscious thought.

So from now on?

Talk back.

Question. Challenge. Replace.

And rewire your brain to work for you—not against you. Because life's too short to spend it arguing with a panicky roommate who lives in your head rent-free.

Chapter 6: The Uncomfortable But Necessary Art of Self-Compassion

Alright, you've gotten pretty good at talking back to anxiety. You've learned how to challenge your thoughts, rewrite the script, and stop treating your brain like it's CNN breaking news. You've assembled an impressive toolkit for questioning those catastrophic predictions and melodramatic interpretations that would make even soap opera writers say, "Whoa, dial it back a bit."

But now? Now we need to address something far more uncomfortable.

How you talk to you.

Because—let's be real—some of y'all are straight-up savage to yourselves.

The kind of mean where, if we recorded your internal monologue and played it at a party, guests would slowly back away from you with concerned expressions. The kind of mean that would get you not just fired but escorted out by security if you spoke to colleagues that way. The kind of mean that would end friendships faster than someone who double-dips at every social gathering.

Like, can you imagine if you heard someone talking to your best friend the way your internal voice talks to you during a regular Tuesday afternoon?

"Wow, you messed that up. Classic you. You're such a failure. You'll probably never get this right. Honestly, I don't know why you even bother trying. Maybe consider a career as a professional disappointment?"

"Oh, great, you embarrassed yourself again. That comment you made in the meeting? Everyone is definitely in a group chat right now, sharing screenshots and laughing about it. You should probably update your LinkedIn before they fire you."

"You should have figured this out by now. You're behind in life. Everyone else has their act together except you. Even your cat judges you when you can't figure out how to assemble IKEA furniture."

"Seriously? You're still struggling with this? What's wrong with you? This should be easy. My grandmother could do this blindfolded while baking cookies and solving world peace."

"Look at you, making the same mistake again. You never learn, do you? This is why you're not where you want to be in life. This is why your high school crush is now married with three perfect children and a house that looks like a Pottery Barn catalog."

If you heard someone saying this to a friend, you'd transform into a protective mama bear faster than you can say "absolutely not." You'd be like, "Excuse me? That is RUDE. Do not talk to them like that. What is wrong with you? They're doing their best while dealing with the crushing weight of existence, inflation, and the fact that every avocado reaches perfect ripeness for approximately 17 minutes."

And yet... when you say it to yourself?

No one stops you. No one steps in. No one calls it out for the abusive language it actually is. Your brain is basically hosting a roast comedy special starring you, except there's no audience laughter—just the soft sound of your self-esteem crumbling.

It's just you, roasting yourself in your own head, completely unchecked. An endless internal monologue of criticism, judgment, and unrealistic standards, with no opposing counsel to object when things get out of hand. Your brain is basically running a 24/7 podcast called "Why You're Not Good Enough" with unlimited episodes and no commercial breaks.

So today? That stops.

Because the truth is:

You can't heal while bullying yourself. You can't grow while constantly tearing yourself down. You will never be "motivated" by self-hatred any more than a plant grows faster if you scream at it about its inadequate photosynthesis skills.

Self-criticism isn't fuel—it's a weight. It doesn't push you forward; it's more like trying to run a marathon with a angry raccoon clinging to your back. It doesn't help you learn; it makes you afraid to try. It doesn't make you stronger; it depletes the emotional resources you need to actually improve, like trying to charge your phone by repeatedly dropping it.

So today, we're going to do something weird, uncomfortable, and wildly effective: Learn to be nice to ourselves. And I promise, this might be the most difficult, most revolutionary, most necessary skill in this entire book. It's like trying to teach a fish to appreciate being out of water—completely unnatural at first, but actually life-changing.

Step 1: Recognizing That Self-Criticism is Not the Same as Self-Improvement (AKA Your Inner Drill Sergeant Needs to Chill)

A lot of people confuse self-compassion with laziness. They've bought into the toxic myth that the only way to achieve anything is through relentless self-criticism and harsh judgment, like your brain is some sort of boot camp instructor from a 1980s movie who needs to break you down before building you up.

They think:

"If I start being nice to myself, I'll lose all motivation and transform into a human-shaped blob of inertia. I need to be hard on myself to achieve my goals, like how Gordon Ramsay yells at chefs to make better risotto."

"If I don't push myself with criticism, I'll never improve. The voice in my head that calls me lazy and worthless is what gets me to the gym. Without it, I'd just stay in bed watching 'Is It Cake?' for 14 hours straight."

"If I go easy on myself, I'll just turn into some unmotivated couch potato who eats snacks and gives up on life. My inner critic is keeping me from becoming a complete failure who lives in a van down by the river."

And let me just say:

THAT. IS. NOT. HOW. THIS. WORKS.

Being kind to yourself doesn't mean you stop growing. It just means you stop treating yourself like that moldy leftover container in the back of your fridge while you grow.

Self-compassion isn't about lowering your standards or giving up on your goals. It's not about making excuses or avoiding accountability. It's about changing the internal environment in which that growth and accountability happen. It's about switching from "punish yourself thin" to "nourish yourself healthy."

Think of it this way: Plants grow better in nutrient-rich soil with adequate water and sunlight. They don't grow better when you scream at them about how they're not tall enough yet or compare them to the neighbor's ficus. Your mind works the same way—it thrives in conditions of support, not under constant criticism. You wouldn't water a plant with Mountain Dew and expect it to thrive, so why feed your brain a steady diet of toxic thoughts?

CHAPTER 6: THE UNCOMFORTABLE BUT NECESSARY ART OF SELF-COMPASSION

Because let's be honest: Self-criticism is not making you better. It's your brain's greatest hits album of terrible remixes called "Songs to Feel Terrible About Yourself To."

Has calling yourself a failure actually helped you succeed? (No, it's probably made you too afraid to try, like refusing to dance because you once fell at your middle school formal.)

Has telling yourself you're not good enough made you feel more capable? (No, it's likely undermined your confidence in your abilities faster than a TikTok trend makes you question your fashion choices.)

Has mentally beating yourself up ever made you happier, stronger, or more confident? (Absolutely not. It's just made you feel awful about yourself, like listening to that one sad song on repeat after a breakup.)

Has telling yourself you're lazy motivated you to be more productive? (No, it's probably made you feel defeated before you even start, like looking at your inbox with 3,427 unread emails.)

Has criticizing your appearance made you healthier? (No, it's likely created a negative relationship with your body and your health that's about as helpful as trying to assemble furniture without instructions.)

Research consistently shows that self-criticism is associated with greater anxiety, depression, and reduced goal progress. It doesn't make you stronger or more disciplined—it actively undermines your ability to cope with setbacks and learn from mistakes. It's like hiring a life coach who just follows you around saying, "You suck at everything" and then expecting to feel motivated.

Self-criticism isn't making you better. It's just making you miserable. It's creating an internal environment of stress, shame, and fear—none of which are conducive to actual learning, growth, or sustained motivation. It's like trying to grow a garden in a toxic waste dump and wondering why nothing blooms.

And you can grow without hating yourself through the process. In fact, you'll likely grow more effectively, more sustainably, and more authentically when you approach yourself with kindness rather than contempt. Think of it as switching from an abusive coach to a supportive one—same goal, way better results, significantly less emotional damage.

Step 2: The "Would You Say This to a Friend?" Test (AKA Don't Be That Friend)

If you take nothing else from this chapter, take this one strategy: It's simple, immediate, and remarkably effective at putting self-talk into perspective. It's the Uno reverse card for your toxic self-talk.

Whenever you catch yourself beating yourself up, stop and ask:

"Would I say this to a friend? Or would they block my number and tell mutual acquaintances I've 'changed'?"

If the answer is no, then you shouldn't be saying it to yourself either. Full stop. No exceptions. Not even if Mercury is in retrograde or if you've had a particularly rough day.

This isn't just a feel-good exercise; it's about correcting a dangerous double standard. Most of us have different rules for how we treat ourselves versus how we treat others. We offer understanding, patience, and compassion to others while denying those same basic courtesies to ourselves. It's like having a "friends eat free" policy at your restaurant but charging yourself triple.

Let's make this concrete with some examples:

Situation: You made a mistake at work.

Your brain: "Wow. You're so incompetent. Everyone knows you're terrible at this. They probably regret hiring you. It's just a matter of time before they figure out you're a fraud and replace you with an AI or a particularly talented golden retriever."

Would you say this to a friend? No. You'd say something supportive and constructive, not suggest they're about to be replaced by a canine.

Better response: "Okay, that wasn't great, but I can learn from it. One mistake doesn't define me or my capabilities. Everyone makes errors sometimes—it's how we improve. Remember when Elon Musk crashed that rocket? And he's still allowed to run companies!"

Situation: You're feeling overwhelmed and behind in life.

Your brain: "Why are you like this? Everyone else has it together but you. You're so disorganized and incapable. You're failing at adulthood while everyone else is thriving. Your college roommate already owns a house and has a retirement plan while you're still trying to figure out how to fold a fitted sheet."

Would you say this to a friend? No. You'd offer perspective and encouragement, not a comparative breakdown of their life failures.

Better response: "I'm doing my best with the resources I have right now. Progress isn't always fast or linear, but it's still progress. And comparison is pointless—I don't actually know what struggles others are facing behind their curated Instagram feeds. For all I know, that 'perfect' friend cries while organizing their sock drawer."

Situation: You look in the mirror and don't like what you see.

Your brain: "Look at you. You're disgusting. No wonder people don't find you attractive. You should be ashamed to leave the house looking like that. Maybe you should just wrap yourself in a blanket like a burrito person for the rest of your life."

Would you say this to a friend? Never. You'd be horrified if someone spoke to your friend that way. You'd probably be planning an elaborate revenge scenario involving glitter bombs.

Better response: "This is the body that carries me through life. It deserves respect regardless of its appearance. My worth isn't determined by societal beauty standards, and I can work toward health without tearing myself down. Besides, in the grand cosmic scheme, we're all just star stuff walking around on a spinning rock—perspective is everything."

Situation: You're struggling to learn a new skill.

Your brain: "You're so stupid. Everyone else picks this up quickly. You'll never get it. Just give up now and save yourself the embarrassment. Remember that time in 4th grade when you couldn't do long division and had to stay after class? This is exactly like that, but you're an adult now, which makes it worse."

Would you say this to a friend? No. You'd encourage them to keep trying and remind them that learning takes time, not bring up traumatic elementary school memories.

Better response: "Learning new things is supposed to be challenging—that's how we know we're growing. My current difficulty isn't a reflection of my intelligence; it's just part of the normal learning process. The neural pathways just haven't formed yet. Even Einstein probably struggled with something... maybe making small talk at parties?"

Seriously—if it's too mean for a friend, then it's too mean for you. You deserve, at minimum, the same basic decency you would offer to someone else. And frankly, since you're the person you spend the most time with (even in the bathroom—especially in the bathroom), shouldn't you aim to be especially kind to yourself?

This isn't about special treatment; it's about ending the unwarranted abuse you've been directing at yourself. It's about becoming the supportive friend you need instead of the cruel bully you've tolerated. It's about firing your brain's toxic podcast host and replacing them with someone who actually wants you to succeed.

Step 3: Rewrite the Script (Turn Self-Criticism into Self-Coaching, Not Self-Roasting)

Most of us don't even realize how negative our self-talk is. It's become so automatic, so habitual, so normalized that we don't even register it as unusual or harmful. It's like background noise—constant, pervasive, and barely noticed despite its significant impact. It's the mental equivalent of having a refrigerator hum that's actually saying "you're terrible" in morse code.

We've been doing it for so long that it just feels normal. We mistake familiarity for truth, habit for necessity. It's like that one weird food combination you grew up eating—peanut butter and pickle sandwiches or ketchup on scrambled eggs—that you assumed was normal until someone looked at you with horror in the company break room.

But the good news? You can rewrite the script. You can change the way you speak to yourself. You can transform your inner critic into an inner coach—someone who challenges you without demeaning you, who pushes you without shaming you, who helps you grow without making you feel worthless. Someone who's less Gordon Ramsay screaming about raw chicken and more Ted Lasso believing in you even when you don't believe in yourself.

Let's take some common self-criticisms and turn them into something actually helpful:

"I'm so stupid." → "I made a mistake, but I can learn from it. Intelligence isn't fixed—it grows through challenges. Even Einstein probably forgot his keys sometimes."

"I'm not good enough." → "I'm doing my best with what I have right now, and that is enough. 'Good enough' isn't a fixed state; it's a moving target. Besides, perfection is boring—even Netflix shows jump the shark eventually."

"I'll never get this right." → "I'm struggling now, but I will figure it out. Mastery takes time and includes plenty of mistakes along the way. Remember when I couldn't figure out how to use the self-checkout and now I'm basically a scanning professional?"

"I always mess up." → "I'm human. Progress is messy. Every expert was once a beginner who kept showing up despite setbacks. Even Taylor Swift probably had uncomfortable dance recitals as a kid."

"I'm such a failure." → "I haven't succeeded at this yet, but that doesn't define me. Failure is an event, not an identity. Thomas Edison failed 1,000 times before inventing the light bulb, and no one remembers him as 'Thomas Edison, Professional Failure.'"

"I'm so lazy." → "I might be struggling with motivation right now, but that doesn't make me lazy. Maybe I need rest, a different approach, or to reconsider if this goal truly aligns with my values. My body might actually be trying to tell me something important, like 'this deadline is made up and sleep is not.'"

"I'm a disappointment." → "I may not have met certain expectations, but I'm not a disappointment as a person. My worth isn't contingent on meeting every expectation. Besides, the unexpected plot twists often make for a better story in the end."

"Everyone else is doing better than me." → "Everyone has their own timeline and challenges. I'm exactly where I need to be on my unique journey. For all I know, that 'successful' person I'm comparing myself to cries in their car during lunch breaks or still doesn't know how tax brackets work."

This isn't about being delusional or pretending everything is perfect. Self-compassion isn't about ignoring problems or avoiding responsibility. It's not about giving yourself a participation trophy for showing up to your own life. It's about acknowledging challenges without attacking your inherent worth as a person.

It's about changing the way you treat yourself so you can actually improve. It's about creating an internal environment conducive to growth, resilience, and genuine confidence—not the fragile facade of confidence that crumbles at the first sign of difficulty, like a chocolate teapot in hot weather.

Think of it as the difference between a terrible coach who screams insults from the sidelines while nursing a hangover and an excellent coach who offers constructive feedback while maintaining belief in your potential. Which one would help you perform better? Which one would you rather have in your corner during difficult times? Which one would you want to grab post-game drinks with?

Step 4: Separate Performance from Worth (You Are Not Your LinkedIn Profile)

One of the most toxic aspects of self-criticism is how it collapses the distinction between what you do and who you are. It confuses your behavior, accomplishments, or appearance with your fundamental value as a human being. It's like thinking your car's worth is determined solely by how clean the cup holders are.

This is a dangerous and false equivalence that creates a never-ending treadmill of achievement and appearance-based worth. It's why:

You feel worthless after a professional setback, as if your job title is tattooed on your soul You feel unlovable when someone rejects you, like your dating app success rate is the measure of your heart You feel like a failure when you make a mistake, as though humans were designed to be error-free robots You feel defective when you struggle with something, forgetting that struggle is literally how growth happens

The truth is, your worth isn't determined by:

How productive you are (you're not an Amazon warehouse) How attractive you are (you're not a Renaissance painting) How successful you are (you're not a spreadsheet) How smart you are (you're not a walking Wikipedia) How likable you are (you're not a golden retriever) How wealthy you are (you're not a Bitcoin)

Your worth is intrinsic. It's not something you earn through achievement or lose through failure. It's not contingent on fitting into society's often arbitrary and shifting standards. It's not something that increases when you succeed or decreases when you fail. You don't become 22% more valuable as a human because you got promoted or 37% less valuable because you got dumped.

This doesn't mean you shouldn't strive for growth or improvement. It means that when you do, it's from a foundation of basic self-respect rather than a desperate attempt to prove your worth through external validation. It's the difference between "I want to improve because I respect myself" and "I need to improve because otherwise I'm worthless."

Try practicing these distinctions:

"I failed at this task" versus "I am a failure" (One is an event, the other is an identity) "I made a mistake" versus "I am a mistake" (One happened, the other implies your birth was unfortunate) "I'm struggling with this" versus "I am inadequate" (One is temporary, the other is a life sentence) "This relationship ended" versus "I am unlovable" (One door closed, not all doors) "I'm having difficulty focusing today" versus "I am lazy" (One is a state, the other is a character assassination)

When you separate performance from worth, you can address problems more effectively because they're not existential threats to your value as a person. You can take risks, make mistakes, and grow without the crushing weight of believing your entire worth is at stake with every action. You can post that selfie without perfect lighting, send that email with a typo, or try that new recipe that might turn out... creative.

Step 5: Progress, Not Perfection (Rome Wasn't Built While Scrolling Instagram)

If you're used to beating yourself up, self-compassion is going to feel weird at first. It might feel uncomfortable, unnatural, or even wrong. You might feel like you're letting yourself off the hook or being self-indulgent. Your brain might panic like, "Wait, if we're not constantly criticizing ourselves, how will we know we're terrible?"

It's like switching from a terrible diet to healthy eating—your brain will resist. There's discomfort in change, even when that change is ultimately beneficial. Your inner critic has been running the show for so long that it won't surrender control without a fight. It's like that one friend who refuses to give up the AUX cord even though they keep playing the same five songs from 2007.

But self-compassion is a muscle. It's a skill that can be developed through consistent practice, not a trait you either have or don't have. It gets stronger with use, weaker with neglect. It's like learning to make your bed every day or resist checking your ex's Instagram—uneasy at first, then second nature.

The more you practice it, the stronger it gets. The more you intentionally replace self-criticism with self-compassion, the more natural it feels. What starts as a conscious effort eventually becomes a habitual way of relating to yourself. The first time you say something kind to yourself, it might feel as clumsy as calling your teacher "Mom" in fifth grade, but eventually, it feels normal.

And no, you won't immediately stop the negative thoughts. Years of mental habits don't disappear overnight. But you can start catching them, questioning them, and choosing better ones. You can interrupt the automatic cycle of self-criticism and begin inserting moments of kindness and understanding. It's like editing a document—you don't have to rewrite the whole thing at once, just start fixing errors as you spot them.

So, moving forward?

No more calling yourself names. You wouldn't tolerate someone calling your friend stupid, worthless, or lazy—not even if they brought cookies afterward to make up for it. Don't tolerate it when directed at yourself.

No more tearing yourself down. Your challenges and struggles don't need the added burden of your own contempt. That's like trying to climb a mountain while actively throwing rocks at yourself.

No more treating yourself like your own worst enemy. You face enough opposition in the world without creating more from within. You're supposed to be on your own team, not heckling yourself from the sidelines.

You don't have to be perfect. You just have to be kinder to yourself than you were yesterday. It's a pretty low bar, really. Baby steps. If your self-talk was previously at "ruthless dictator" levels, aim for "stern but fair substitute teacher" before working up to "supportive coach."

Because that's how real change happens. Not through overnight transformation, but through consistent small choices that gradually shift your relationship with yourself. It's like building a playlist one song at a time until you've completely changed the soundtrack of your life.

Start with just noticing the negative self-talk. "Oh, there's my brain being a jerk again. Interesting." Then work on questioning it. "Is that actually true, or is my brain catastrophizing like it's being paid by the disaster?" Then try replacing it with something more compassionate. "I'm doing my best with what I know right now, and I can always learn more." It's a process, not an event. Give yourself permission to be a beginner at this.

Step 6: Develop Self-Compassion Rituals (Beyond Just Buying Yourself Plants)

Sometimes, especially when you're in the grip of intense self-criticism, trying to think your way into self-compassion doesn't work well. It's like trying to think yourself calm during a panic attack or logic yourself out of heartbreak. In those moments, having concrete practices—actual things you can do—can be more effective than trying to change your thoughts directly.

Consider developing self-compassion rituals that you can turn to when your inner critic is particularly loud and sounds suspiciously like that one relative who always comments on your weight at holiday gatherings:

Physical self-compassion: Place your hand on your heart or give yourself a gentle hug. This activates your body's caregiving response and can help shift you out of fight-or-flight mode. Yes, it feels silly at first. Do it anyway. Your nervous system doesn't care if you feel clumsy.

Written self-compassion: Keep a self-compassion journal where you write what you'd say to a friend facing your current situation. Sometimes seeing these words on paper has more impact than just thinking them. Plus, it's hard to argue with yourself when you've literally written down the evidence of your unreasonable standards.

Verbal self-compassion: Develop a few go-to phrases that you can say out loud to yourself: "This is a moment of suffering. Suffering is part of life. May I be kind to myself in this moment." Or the shorter version: "This sucks. Everyone struggles sometimes. I've got my own back." Bonus points if you say it in a gentle, slightly British accent like a meditation app.

Environmental self-compassion: Create spaces in your home that communicate care and respect for yourself—whether it's a comfortable reading nook, a tidy workspace, or simply making your bed each morning. Your physical environment sends signals to your brain about how you deserve to be treated. If your car is cleaner than your bedroom, that's data worth examining.

Boundary self-compassion: Practice saying no to things that overextend you and yes to things that nurture you. Setting appropriate boundaries is a concrete expression of self-respect. Remember: "No" is a complete sentence. You don't need to provide a 12-paragraph explanation for why you can't attend your third cousin's dog's birthday party.

These rituals can serve as pattern interrupts when you're caught in a spiral of self-criticism. They provide concrete actions you can take even when your emotions are overwhelming, giving you a pathway back to self-compassion when you need it most. Think of them as emergency break-glass procedures for when your mind is being particularly unkind.

If You're Going to Live in Your Own Head, Make It a Nice Place to Be (Not a Horror Movie)

Here's the reality:

You're stuck with yourself for life. There's no escaping the relationship you have with yourself. No matter where you go, what you achieve, or who else comes into your life, you will always be there, talking to yourself, interpreting events, shaping your experience. You are your own permanent roommate who never pays rent on time.

You live in your own head 24/7. You'll spend more time with yourself than with any other person on the planet. Your internal dialogue is the most persistent, consistent voice you will ever hear. It's like being married to yourself, except there's no option for divorce or even a trial separation.

So why would you make it a toxic, hostile place to be? Why would you choose to live with a bully, a critic, a voice that constantly tears you down and points out your flaws? What purpose does that serve, other than to make your one and only life more difficult and painful than it needs to be? It's like choosing to live with someone who leaves passive-aggressive notes on the fridge about how you breathe too loudly.

Start talking to yourself the way you talk to the people you love. Start treating yourself with grace, patience, and kindness. Start cheering yourself on instead of tearing yourself down. Be the supportive friend you need in your own head. Be the person who brings cookies and says, "This is hard, but you're doing great."

This isn't self-indulgence; it's self-preservation. It's not weakness; it's wisdom. It's recognizing that the relationship you have with yourself is the foundation for every other relationship in your life, and that foundation deserves to be solid, supportive, and sustainable. You wouldn't build a house on quicksand; don't build your life on self-hatred.

Because at the end of the day?

You are doing better than you think. You are growing in ways you don't even realize. And you deserve the same compassion you so freely give to everyone else. You wouldn't let your best friend talk to themselves the way you talk to yourself, so why allow it in your own head?

Not because you've earned it through some special achievement. Not because you're perfect or never make mistakes. But because you're human, and that alone is enough to warrant basic kindness. The bar is literally on the ground here: be as nice to yourself as you would be to a stranger who dropped their coffee at Starbucks.

So start today. Catch one self-critical thought and replace it with something more compassionate. Extend to yourself the same courtesy you'd give to a friend. Begin the practice of treating yourself like someone worthy of respect and care.

Because you are. And it's about time your internal dialogue reflected that truth instead of sounding like a disappointed parent reviewing your life choices.

After all, if you wouldn't accept this treatment from others, why accept it from yourself? You deserve better from the one person who'll be with you through every moment of your life. That person might as well be kind.

PART 3: COPING STRATEGIES – BECAUSE YOU CAN'T JUST THINK YOUR WAY OUT OF EVERYTHING

Knowledge is great, but without action, it's about as useful as an umbrella in a hurricane. This section is where the rubber meets the road—practical strategies to manage anxiety when it shows up uninvited (which it will, repeatedly, like that relative who always crashes on your couch).

We'll explore why doing things while scared is better than waiting to feel brave, how externalizing your thoughts deflates their power faster than poking a balloon, and why humor might just be your secret weapon against anxiety.

Consider this your emergency toolkit for when anxiety strikes—because knowing why your brain acts like a overreaction queen is one thing, but having actual strategies to deal with it in the moment? That's where the real magic happens.

Chapter 7: Action > Anxiety

What If I Just... Did the Thing Anyway? (A Radical Approach to Getting Stuff Done While Your Brain Screams 'No Thanks')

Why Doing Things Scares You, But Also Saves You

What If The Best Way to Beat Anxiety... Is to Stop Waiting to Feel Ready?

Alright, deep breath, because this one might sting a little—like applying hand sanitizer to a paper cut, it hurts but it's good for you.

If you're someone who struggles with anxiety, there's a good chance you do something I like to call "overthinking everything to death and then not doing anything at all." It's like mental quicksand—the more you think, the deeper you sink, until eventually, you're too paralyzed to move at all, trapped in a prison of your own making, furnished with excuses and decorated with "what-ifs."

You think about going to the gym, but then overanalyze it until you talk yourself out of it. "What if I look stupid? What if people judge me? What if I don't know how to use the equipment? Maybe I should research proper gym etiquette for another week. Actually, I should probably watch 47 YouTube videos about proper form first. Or maybe I'll just start next Monday instead. Monday is definitely the optimal day to begin new habits. Next Monday, though. Not this one."

You want to text someone first, but spend so much time debating the perfect wording that you never send it. "Is this too casual? Too formal? Too eager? Not eager enough? Should I use an emoji? Which emoji? Does the laughing-crying face make me look desperate? Maybe I should wait for them to text me first. But what if they're waiting for me to text first? This is exhausting. Maybe I'll just wait another day and see what happens. Or I could re-draft it for the 17th time..."

You have a project you need to start, but your brain convinces you to just think about it for a few more weeks instead. "I need to plan this perfectly. I need to account for every possible obstacle. I need to feel completely prepared and completely motivated. I need to wait for that magical moment when the stars align, my energy levels are optimal, my schedule is completely clear, and no other human needs anything from me. I'll start when I feel ready." (Narrator: They never felt ready.)

This is called analysis paralysis, and it's anxiety's favorite weapon. It's not just a quirky personality trait that makes for good self-deprecating jokes at dinner parties—it's a sophisticated defense mechanism your brain uses to avoid potential discomfort, risk, or failure. By overthinking, your brain creates the illusion of productivity while actually keeping you safely in your comfort zone, wrapped in a cozy blanket of procrastination and "research."

Because anxiety doesn't just make you feel bad—it makes you avoid things. It's like having an overprotective helicopter parent living in your head, one who's convinced that the world is full of dangers and you're never quite prepared enough to face them. It convinces you that thinking about something is the same as doing it, that preparation is the same as action, that intentions are the same as results. (Spoiler alert: They're not. Not even close. Not even in the same galaxy.)

But here's the biggest truth about anxiety that nobody likes to hear:

The only way to get rid of anxiety about something... is to actually do the thing.
Not think about it. Not plan it perfectly. Not wait until you feel 100% ready.
Just. Do. The. Thing.

And yes, I know, this sounds terrible. It's probably the last thing you want to hear. Your brain is probably already listing all the reasons why this advice doesn't apply to you specifically, or why it's not that simple, or why you need to wait just a little longer. It's creating a PowerPoint presentation titled "Why That's Actually Impossible For Me Specifically: A 47-Slide Explanation" complete with charts, graphs, and emotional testimonials from your past failures.

But let me explain why this works. Not just in theory, but in practice—in the messy, real-world psychological trenches where anxiety lives and breathes and throws temper tantrums like a toddler who's been told they can't have a third cookie.

Step 1: The Anxiety Cycle (And How to Break It)

Anxiety follows a predictable pattern. It's almost mathematical in its reliability, like a formula that produces the same result every time, or like that one friend who always, without fail, suggests the same restaurant every time you ask where to eat.

1. You feel anxious about something. Your heart races like it's competing in the Kentucky Derby, your palms sweat like they're trying to solve climate change one handshake at a time, your stomach churns like it's making artisanal butter, and your mind fills with worst-case scenarios that would make apocalyptic movies look optimistic.

2. You avoid it to make the anxiety go away. You cancel plans, procrastinate, make excuses that would impress a creative writing professor ("I can't go to the party because my cousin's neighbor's dog is feeling sad and needs emotional support"), or distract yourself with easier, more comfortable activities like reorganizing your sock drawer by color, thickness, and emotional significance.

3. You feel temporary relief because you avoided it. The physical symptoms subside. The mental alarm bells quiet down. You feel better—for now. Your brain gives you a little dopamine cookie as a reward for staying "safe."

4. Your brain learns, "Oh, avoiding things makes me feel better. Avoidance = safety. Let me remember that for next time." Your brain, being the efficient pattern-recognition machine that it is, makes note of what worked to reduce discomfort, filing it away like a squirrel hoarding nuts for winter.

5. The next time anxiety shows up, it feels even stronger. Because now your brain has evidence that the thing is dangerous (why else would you have avoided it?), and it has proof that avoidance works. So it doubles down on both the anxiety signal and the avoidance recommendation, like a marketing team that found a successful campaign and decides to increase the budget.

This is how procrastination, avoidance, and social anxiety get worse over time. It's not random, and it's not a character flaw. It's a predictable psychological pattern created by an overprotective brain that's trying to keep you safe—but is actually keeping you stuck, like a well-meaning friend who keeps talking you out of going on dates because they're worried you might get hurt, leaving you perpetually single but "safe."

The more you avoid something, the scarier it feels. Each time you step back from the edge, your brain becomes more convinced that whatever lies beyond that edge must be truly dangerous, like a tiger or a tax audit or someone asking you to explain cryptocurrency at a dinner party. The fear compounds, the avoidance strengthens, and the cycle perpetuates itself like a never-ending season of a show that should have been canceled years ago.

And there is only one way to break this cycle:

You have to do the thing anyway.

Even while you feel anxious. Not after the anxiety subsides, not when you feel "ready," not when Mercury is in retrograde and the moon is full and you've had exactly the right amount of coffee, but right in the midst of the discomfort, while your palms are still sweaty and your heart is still racing.

Even while your brain is screaming. While it's telling you all the reasons why you should wait, why you're not prepared, why this is a terrible idea, why you should probably just check your phone one more time before starting.

Even when every fiber of your being wants to run in the opposite direction. When avoidance feels like the most natural, most sensible response in the world, like leaving a building that's on fire or declining to pet a growling dog.

Because when you face it head-on, something incredible happens:

Your brain learns. It collects new evidence that contradicts its catastrophic predictions, like a scientist who's forced to revise a hypothesis when new data emerges. It registers that you survived, that the worst didn't happen, that the discomfort was temporary—like a wave that peaks and then recedes rather than the tsunami your anxiety predicted.

Your brain realizes you can handle it. Not just theoretically, but experientially. You've proven to yourself that you're more capable than your anxiety led you to believe, like someone who's been told they can't run a mile their whole life suddenly doing it.

And next time? It's a little easier. The anxiety might still show up, like an unwanted guest at a party, but it doesn't feel quite as overwhelming. The urge to avoid doesn't grip you quite as tightly. The step forward doesn't require quite as much courage. It's like building a muscle—the first rep is the hardest, but it gets easier with consistent practice.

This is exposure therapy in its most basic form—confronting what scares you until it doesn't scare you as much anymore. Not because the thing changed, but because you changed your relationship to it. You're still you, it's still the thing, but the space between you has been transformed.

Step 2: The "Feelings vs. Actions" Rule

Most people assume that actions follow feelings. This seems intuitive, almost self-evident, like assuming that rain follows clouds or that regret follows texting your ex at 2 AM. Surely, you need to feel a certain way before you can act a certain way, right?

They think:

"Once I feel confident, I'll start that business." (As if confidence is a prerequisite rather than a result.)

"Once I feel motivated, I'll begin that project." (As if motivation is something that arrives like an Amazon package rather than something generated through action.)

"Once I stop feeling anxious, I'll take the risk." (As if anxiety is something you can wait out, like a summer storm or a bad haircut.)

"Once I feel ready, I'll make the change." (As if "ready" is a definable state rather than a moving target that recedes as you approach it.)

"Once I feel inspired, I'll write that book." (As if inspiration is something that strikes from the heavens rather than something cultivated through consistent practice.)

WRONG.

That's not how this works. That's not how any of this works. That's not how human psychology actually functions in the real world. It's like waiting to get hungry before you go grocery shopping—by the time you feel it, you're already in trouble.

Because in reality?

You don't wait until you feel confident. You do the thing first, and then confidence follows. You develop confidence through action, through accumulated experiences of doing things despite uncertainty, through proving to yourself that you can handle challenges. Confidence isn't the prerequisite—it's the prize you get for taking action anyway.

You don't wait until you feel motivated. You start, and then motivation kicks in. Motivation isn't a prerequisite for action; it's often a result of action. The simple act of beginning creates momentum that generates its own motivation, like a car that's easier to steer once it's already moving.

You don't wait until the fear disappears. You take action, and fear shrinks because you proved it wrong. Fear doesn't dissipate through thinking or waiting or scrolling on your phone; it diminishes through direct confrontation that provides contradictory evidence. It's like a schoolyard bully who backs down when someone finally stands up to them.

Feelings follow actions—not the other way around. This isn't just a catchy phrase for Instagram captions; it's a fundamental psychological principle that can transform your relationship with anxiety.

Think about learning to drive. Did you feel completely confident before your first time behind the wheel? Of course not. You probably felt like an impostor in a driver's seat, a child playing a grown-up game, moments away from certain disaster. You felt nervous, uncomfortable, overwhelmed by all the things you had to remember. But you did it anyway, and gradually, through repeated action, the confidence came. Now you probably drive while eating a burrito and singing along to the radio without giving it a second thought.

Or think about public speaking. Even experienced speakers often feel nervous before taking the stage. They don't wait until the nervousness disappears before walking up to the microphone; they walk up to the microphone with sweaty palms and a dry mouth, and the nervousness eventually subsides as they get into their presentation. They use the adrenaline rather than waiting for it to go away.

If you wait until you feel ready, you will be waiting forever. Readiness isn't a state that magically arrives if you wait long enough, like a bus at a station or the perfect ripeness of an avocado; it's a state you create through action, through starting before you feel prepared, through doing things while they still scare you.

The implication is both challenging and liberating: You don't need to feel good to get going. You need to get going to start feeling good. It's like jumping into a cold pool—the anticipation is worse than the actual experience, and once you're in, your body adjusts.

Step 3: The "5-Second Rule" (Because Thinking is Your Enemy)

You know what kills more dreams than failure?

Overthinking.

More specifically, the gap between impulse and action—that crucial moment when you have an instinct to do something positive but then give your brain time to talk you out of it, like letting a pessimistic friend review your dating profile before you post it. That hesitation, that pause, that "let me think about this" moment is where anxiety does its most insidious work, whispering all the reasons why you should wait, why you're not ready, why the timing isn't right.

So, let's introduce a game-changing strategy:

The 5-Second Rule

(Not the one about dropping food. A better one, though I won't judge you for eating that cookie that touched the counter for 4.9 seconds.)

This rule comes from Mel Robbins, and it's ridiculously simple:

The moment you feel the urge to do something but hesitate, count down from 5.

5... 4... 3... 2... 1... MOVE.

Send the text. Don't reread it seventeen times like you're proofreading your college thesis. Don't overthink it. Don't worry about every possible interpretation of your words, or whether your period seems passive-aggressive, or if "haha" seems too casual while "hahaha" seems too eager.

Start the task. Don't wait for the perfect moment, when the lighting is perfect and the mood is right and the planets are aligned, like you're waiting to take an Instagram photo rather than just doing your taxes. Don't break it down into smaller and smaller steps until you've convinced yourself it's too complicated and maybe you need a PhD before you can begin.

Walk into the gym. Don't debate whether today is the right day, or if your outfit is optimally slimming, or if you'll be the only one who doesn't know what they're doing. Don't worry about what to wear or who might be watching or whether you'll know what to do. Just go, with your imperfect outfit and your imperfect knowledge and your imperfect body.

Speak up in the meeting. Don't rehearse your comment until the moment has passed and the topic has changed and now you'd have to uneasily redirect the conversation. Don't convince yourself that someone else will make the same point or that your idea isn't revolutionary enough to share.

Why?

Because hesitation is the death of action. It's the gap where doubt creeps in, where anxiety builds its case, where your brain manufactures reasons to stay comfortable and safe, like a lawyer presenting evidence for why you should definitely stay on the couch.

If you let your brain think about something for too long, it will find ten reasons why you should just stay where you are. It's remarkably creative when it comes to generating excuses, alternative plans, and worst-case scenarios—anything to keep you in your comfort zone. Your brain could win awards for the elaborate stories it creates about why now isn't the right time, like a novelist who specializes in tales of procrastination.

So don't give it time.

Just count down, and do the thing. Physically move your body before your brain has a chance to intervene. Create action before doubt can create paralysis. It's like ripping off a Band-Aid instead of slowly peeling it—sometimes the quick approach is less painful overall.

This might sound simplistic, like I'm suggesting you can solve complex psychological issues with a kindergarten countdown, but it's based on solid neuroscience. When you count down, you're essentially interrupting the habit loop in your brain. You're breaking the automatic pattern of hesitation followed by rationalization followed by inaction. You're inserting a new routine that bypasses the overthinking stage entirely, like a secret shortcut that lets you skip past the anxiety checkpoint.

It doesn't eliminate anxiety—nothing does—but it prevents anxiety from stopping you in your tracks. And over time, as you accumulate experiences of taking action despite fear, the anxiety itself begins to lose its grip, like a muscle that atrophies from disuse.

Step 4: Shrinking Anxiety Through Exposure Therapy

Another reason action beats anxiety?

Because the more you do something, the less scary it becomes. This isn't wishful thinking or Instagram inspiration wrapped in a sunset filter; it's one of the most well-established principles in psychology, with more research backing it than most of the "facts" we accept without question.

This is called exposure therapy, and it is the gold standard for treating anxiety. It's what clinicians use to treat phobias, social anxiety, PTSD, and numerous other anxiety disorders—because it works, consistently and reliably, like gravity or the tendency of cats to knock things off tables.

Afraid of talking to people? Talk to people more often, starting small and working your way up from the cashier at the grocery store to the attractive person at the coffee shop. Each interaction becomes a data point proving that social interaction isn't as dangerous as your anxiety suggests, that strangers aren't as judgmental as you fear, that you're not as uneasy as you think.

Afraid of driving? Get in the car more often, perhaps starting with quiet neighborhoods before tackling highways and busy intersections. Each successful journey demonstrates that you can navigate roads safely, building confidence through accumulated experience, until eventually, you're belting out show tunes while cruising down the highway.

Afraid of failure? Start doing things that have a chance of failing—small things at first, then larger ones as your resilience grows. Each attempt—whether it succeeds or fails—shows that you can survive imperfection, that mistakes aren't catastrophic, that there's life after failure. Maybe you apply for a job you're not fully qualified for, or try a recipe that looks complicated, or ask someone out who seems slightly out of your league.

Afraid of heights? Gradually expose yourself to increasingly high places. Start with a step stool, then a ladder, then perhaps a balcony, then a tall building with a view. With each step, your brain gathers evidence that heights aren't automatically deadly, that railings exist for a reason, that the ground stays firmly below you even when you're above it.

Yes, it sucks at first. The discomfort is real, like the muscle soreness that follows a good workout. Exposure therapy isn't about denying your anxiety or pretending you're fine when you're not; it's about acknowledging the discomfort while moving forward anyway.

Yes, it feels uncomfortable, like wearing new shoes or having a difficult conversation. Your body might respond with all the physical symptoms of anxiety—racing heart, sweaty palms, shallow breathing, churning stomach, a general sense that death is imminent despite all evidence to the contrary.

Yes, your brain will scream. It will list every possible danger, remind you of past failures, urge you to retreat to safety, promise to never judge you if you just turn back now. It will narrate worst-case scenarios with the creative flair of a thriller writer working on a deadline. "What if you faint? What if you embarrass yourself? What if everyone laughs? What if you forget how to speak English mid-sentence and can only communicate in dolphin noises?"

But the more you face the thing, the less anxiety you'll have about it. This is because anxiety thrives on the unknown, on the untested, on threats that remain theoretical rather than experienced, like a monster under the bed that disappears when you actually look.

With each exposure, your brain learns that it's survivable. The situation, which once loomed as a vague and terrifying possibility, becomes concrete and manageable, like a shadow that looked like a lurking figure until you turned on the light. Your nervous system, which initially responded with alarm, gradually recalibrates to recognize that this particular stimulus isn't a threat after all, just like a car alarm that eventually stops going off at every slight vibration.

Exposure doesn't need to be extreme or overwhelming. In fact, it works best when it's gradual and manageable—challenging enough to generate some anxiety, but not so overwhelming that you're completely flooded by fear. This is called "optimal arousal" in psychology—the sweet spot where growth happens, like calibrating the difficulty level in a video game so it's challenging enough to be engaging but not so hard that you rage-quit.

Think of it as systematically teaching your brain that the things it fears aren't actually dangerous. Not through argument or rationalization, which is like trying to reason with a toddler having a meltdown, but through direct experience, which is always the most powerful teacher, like letting the toddler discover for themselves that the broccoli isn't actually poisonous.

Step 5: The Magic of Small Wins (Because Momentum is Everything)

You don't need to conquer your biggest fear today.

You just need to start with one small action. Something manageable, something doable, something that stretches you but doesn't break you, like a gentle yoga pose rather than an Olympic gymnastics routine.

Because action creates momentum. It generates energy, confidence, and forward motion that can carry you through subsequent challenges, like a snowball rolling downhill that gathers mass and speed.

And once you get moving, it's easier to keep going. This is Newton's First Law applied to psychology: an object in motion tends to stay in motion. The hardest part is often just starting—like getting out of a warm bed on a cold morning or writing the first sentence of an essay.

So, let's say you're struggling with anxiety about:

Public Speaking: Don't sign up to give a TED Talk in front of thousands of people with millions more watching online. Start by talking more in small conversations. Ask a question in a meeting where you usually stay silent. Contribute a comment in a small group discussion. Volunteer to give a brief update on your part of a project. Gradually increase the number of people you're comfortable speaking in front of, like training for a marathon by starting with a walk around the block.

The Gym: Don't start with a two-hour workout designed by some Instagram fitness influencer who's been training since the womb. Just walk in, do five minutes, and leave. Seriously. Just getting through the door is a win when anxiety has been keeping you on your couch. Next time, stay for ten minutes. Then fifteen. Build gradually until the gym feels like a place where you belong, or at least a place where you don't feel like an impostor who's about to be exposed and ejected.

Social Anxiety: Don't force yourself into a huge event where you'll be surrounded by strangers for hours with no escape route. Just make eye contact and say hello to one person. Maybe it's a cashier, a barista, or someone else whose job includes interacting with you. Then try a brief conversation with a neighbor or colleague. Then perhaps a one-on-one coffee with an acquaintance you'd like to know better. Build up to larger gatherings over time, collecting evidence of your social competence along the way.

Job Applications: Don't try to apply for twenty positions in one day, burning yourself out and ensuring that your twentieth application has the quality and attention to detail of a toddler's finger painting. Start by updating one section of your resume. Then draft a cover letter template. Then research one company you'd like to work for. Then submit one application. Each step is a victory, a data point, a building block for the confidence you need to continue.

Small wins lead to big confidence. They accumulate, building both skill and self-efficacy, like pennies that eventually become dollars. They create a positive feedback loop where success breeds success, where each achievement—no matter how minor it might seem—becomes evidence of your capability, an entry in the "I Can Do Hard Things" column of your mental ledger.

But you have to start. No strategy, no technique, no approach works unless you actually implement it. The smallest action is infinitely more valuable than the grandest intention, just as a single step forward gets you closer to your destination than a thousand imaginary journeys planned in your head.

Step 6: Embrace Imperfect Action

Perfectionism and anxiety are often partners in crime, like peanut butter and jelly if the sandwich made you miserable instead of satisfied. They work together to keep you frozen, convincing you that unless you can do something flawlessly, you shouldn't do it at all, like refusing to sing unless you can hit every note like a professional or declining to drive unless you can race like an F1 champion.

This is a trap. A deadly one that prevents growth, stifles creativity, and nurtures anxiety, like a garden where nothing grows because the gardener is waiting for perfect weather conditions that never arrive.

Instead, embrace what some call "imperfect action"—doing things messily, clumsily, or incompletely, but doing them nonetheless. This approach values progress over perfection, movement over mastery, beginnings over flawless execution, like celebrating the child's first wobbly steps instead of criticizing their lack of marathon-running ability.

When you take imperfect action:

You learn more quickly because you're getting real feedback instead of imagining scenarios, like actually testing a recipe rather than just reading about cooking techniques.

You build resilience because you discover that mistakes aren't fatal, that embarrassment doesn't kill you, that failure is survivable—like a child who falls while learning to walk but gets back up and tries again.

You develop skills through practice rather than theory, like actually playing the guitar instead of watching videos about proper finger positioning.

You reduce anxiety because you're proving that imperfection is survivable, that "good enough" is actually enough, that the world doesn't end when you mess up—like someone who finds out that public speaking doesn't actually cause death.

Think of it this way: A rough draft that exists is infinitely more valuable than a perfect manuscript that remains only in your mind, like a cake that's been baked versus an imaginary gourmet dessert. An clumsy conversation that actually happens teaches you more than a hundred imagined smooth interactions that never occur. A business that launches with flaws has potential; a business plan that stays pristine on paper has none.

The willingness to be bad at something temporarily is often the price of admission for eventually becoming good at it, like the toddler phase of language acquisition that precedes fluency. The willingness to feel uncomfortable is the pathway to growth, like the soreness that precedes muscle development.

So lower the bar. Not on your ultimate goals, but on what constitutes acceptable action today. Give yourself permission to be a beginner, to be clumsy, to not know what you're doing, to make mistakes that make you cringe. What matters is that you're moving forward, however imperfectly, like a hiker who makes progress on a trail even if they're not setting speed records.

You Don't Have to Be Fearless. You Just Have to Act Anyway.

Here's the truth:

Fear is normal. It's a natural human response to uncertainty, to challenge, to situations where outcomes aren't guaranteed, like shivering in cold weather or sweating in heat. Everyone experiences it, from the CEO to the intern, from the seasoned performer to the first-timer.

Anxiety is normal. It's your brain's early warning system, designed to alert you to potential threats, to prepare your body for challenges, to keep you safe in an uncertain world. It's a feature, not a bug—even if it sometimes misfires or overreacts, like a smoke detector that goes off when you're just making toast.

Doubt is normal. It's natural to question yourself, to wonder if you're prepared enough, skilled enough, or worthy enough, to second-guess decisions and replay conversations. Uncertainty is part of the human condition, as universal as hunger or fatigue.

But action?

Action is the only thing that will actually change your life. Not thinking, not planning, not waiting, not wishing, not researching, not preparing—doing. Taking steps, making moves, creating momentum, generating evidence that contradicts your fears, like actually walking through the door instead of just standing outside contemplating the architecture.

So don't wait until you feel brave. Courage isn't the absence of fear; it's acting despite fear. It's feeling the trembling in your hands and reaching out anyway, like the person who asks a question even though their voice shakes.

Don't wait until you feel confident. Confidence comes from repeatedly doing things that scare you and surviving. It's built through action, not acquired through contemplation, like a callus that forms after repeated friction rather than by thinking about friction.

Don't wait until you feel motivated. Motivation is fickle and unreliable, like a friend who says they'll help you move but cancels at the last minute. Discipline—the ability to take action regardless of how you feel—is what creates consistent progress, like the writer who produces pages even on days when inspiration is nowhere to be found.

Just start.

Do something. Anything. Take one small step in the direction of what matters to you, even if your anxiety is screaming like a car alarm at 3 AM, even if doubt is clouding your mind like fog on a window, even if fear is making your heart race like a hamster on an espresso binge.

Because the best way to prove anxiety wrong is to take action while you're still scared. To demonstrate, not through argument but through experience, that you can feel anxious and still function, that you can doubt yourself and still achieve, that you can fear failure and still try, like the swimmer who enters the cold water despite the initial shock and finds that their body adjusts.

And one day, you'll realize—you don't feel as scared anymore. Not because the challenges have disappeared, but because you've grown stronger through facing them, like muscles that develop through resistance. Not because anxiety has vanished completely, but because you've learned that it doesn't get to dictate your choices, that it's just weather in your internal landscape, not the landscape itself.

You've discovered that on the other side of anxiety-inducing action is a version of yourself who is more resilient, more capable, and more free than you ever imagined possible, like someone who learns to swim and suddenly has access to oceans, lakes, and rivers they previously could only admire from shore.

It starts with one step. One action. One moment of doing despite feeling afraid.

What will yours be?

CHAPTER 8: EXTERNALIZING THE CRAZY

SAYING IT OUT LOUD MAKES IT SOUND WAY DUMBER" (YOUR BRAIN'S GREATEST HITS ALBUM OF TERRIBLE REMIXES)

Ever Said Your Anxious Thoughts Out Loud? It's... Embarrassing.

Let's do a quick exercise.

Think of one of the worst anxious thoughts you've had recently. You know, the kind that had you spiraling, sweating, and contemplating a melodramatic life change like moving to a remote cabin in Montana with spotty WiFi and excellent hiking trails. The kind that felt absolutely true and deeply significant in the moment—like finding a suspicious mole that WebMD convinced you was definitely cancer but turned out to be a chocolate chip you didn't realize was stuck to your arm. Got it?

Now, say it out loud.

Really. Right now. Actually form the words with your mouth and let them hang in the air of whatever room you're sitting in, where they can mingle with the dust particles and that weird smell coming from somewhere you can't identify.

You probably don't want to, because deep down, you already know what's about to happen.

The second you say it out loud, it sounds ridiculous. Like hearing your own voice in a recording and thinking, "Do I really sound like THAT?"

Suddenly, "Everyone probably hates me because I texted 'okay' instead of 'ok'" doesn't hold up so well under scrutiny. It's like accusing someone of a federal crime for choosing paper over plastic at the grocery store. "I'm definitely going to fail this presentation and then get fired and then never find another job and end up living in my car" loses some of its convincing power when it has to travel through your actual vocal cords and faces the harsh reality of the physical world, where your cat just looks at you like, "Really? That's what's keeping you up at night? I lick my own butt and sleep 18 hours a day, and I'm doing fine."

This is one of the most underrated tools for dealing with anxiety: Externalizing your thoughts. Taking what feels enormous and overwhelming inside your head—like trying to fit an entire IKEA furniture store into a studio apartment—and bringing it into the physical world where you can actually examine it objectively.

Because when you keep them in your head? They feel huge. They feel undeniable. They feel like the absolute truth whispered directly to you by the universe itself. They have the weight and authority of internal experience, with no opposing viewpoint to challenge them—like having a conspiracy theorist with a podcast broadcasting 24/7 directly into your brain with no "unsubscribe" button.

But the second you write them down, say them out loud, or—best case scenario—laugh about them?

They shrink. They become just one perspective among many, like realizing your "enormous problem" is actually just a Chihuahua in a monster costume. They transform from THE TRUTH to simply a thought—and often, not a very logical one. More like the drunk guy at the party who insists he can definitely do a backflip off the balcony.

So today, we're talking about the three best ways to drag your anxious thoughts into the light so they stop controlling you:

1. Writing them down.

2. Saying them out loud.

3. Making fun of them.

None of these techniques require special training, expensive equipment, or even much time. You won't need to download a $9.99 app with in-app purchases to unlock the "premium anxiety-fighting features." But they're remarkably effective at deflating anxiety's power by removing it from the shadowy realm of your mind and exposing it to the clarifying light of external reality—like finding out the scary urban legend that's been terrifying you is actually just the plot of a mediocre Netflix show everyone stopped talking about three years ago.

Step 1: Writing It Down (Because Your Brain is a Messy Office Desk Operated by a Squirrel on Espresso)

Your brain is a chaotic storage unit packed full of every single worry, memory, unfinished to-do list, and uneasy conversation you've ever had. It's like that drawer in your kitchen where you toss everything that doesn't have a proper place—receipts, batteries, random screws, takeout menus from 2015, that one IKEA Allen wrench you're convinced you'll need someday—but infinitely larger and more disorganized, as if organized by a toddler during a sugar rush.

And instead of organizing this mess, your brain just shoves new anxious thoughts on top of the pile like some kind of hoarder who refuses to throw anything away because "it might be valuable someday." It accumulates concerns without resolution, questions without answers, worries without perspective, like a person who subscribes to every streaming service but never cancels any of them.

This is why anxiety can feel overwhelming.

There's just too much happening up there. Too many unprocessed thoughts swirling around, colliding with each other, amplifying each other. Your mind becomes a crowded, noisy room where you can't hear yourself think clearly—like trying to have a philosophical discussion in the middle of a toddler's birthday party at Chuck E. Cheese.

But the second you write things down? It's like finally clearing space in your mental filing cabinet. It's taking all those loose papers scattered across your mental desktop and putting them neatly into folders where you can actually see what you're dealing with. It's like Marie Kondo walked into your brain and said, "This thought does not spark joy. Thank it and let it go."

Why This Works

It gets the thought OUT of your head. Your brain stops running the same anxious thought on repeat when you physically put it somewhere else. It's like extracting a splinter—once it's out, the irritation begins to subside. Or like finally getting that "Baby Shark" song out of your head by playing literally any other song. Research in neuroscience backs this up: writing activates different neural pathways than thinking, effectively giving your anxiety circuits a break, like unplugging your overheating laptop and letting it cool down.

It makes the thought look smaller. What felt like a huge, catastrophic problem now just looks like... words on a page. There's something profoundly demystifying about seeing your greatest fears reduced to a few sentences in black and white. Inside your head, anxiety has unlimited space to expand like an invasive species with no natural predators; on paper, it's constrained by the physical limitations of words, forced to live in a studio apartment instead of the mansion it had built in your mind.

It forces you to actually look at the thought. Instead of just feeling anxious, you can now analyze what's actually going on, like having security camera footage of a noise you heard at night instead of just lying there imagining increasingly elaborate home invasion scenarios. Writing requires clarification and specificity. Vague feelings like "everything is terrible" must be translated into concrete concerns, which are immediately more manageable. You can't solve a problem you haven't defined, just like you can't fix "my car is making a weird noise" without figuring out which weird noise and where it's coming from.

It creates distance between you and the thought. When it's on paper, it's no longer inseparable from your consciousness. It becomes an object you can observe rather than an experience that consumes you, like the difference between being caught in a tsunami versus watching one on TV. This distance is crucial for developing perspective.

How to Do It

1. **Grab a piece of paper (or your Notes app).** Use whatever's convenient, but there's something particularly effective about handwriting. The physical act of forming letters engages different parts of your brain and can be especially grounding when anxiety has you spiraling, like grabbing onto something solid when you feel like you're falling.

2. **Write down exactly what's bothering you.**

    - Not a cleaned-up version. Not a "reasonable" version. Write down exactly what your brain is saying, like transcribing the world's most overreactiontic podcast host.

    - Include the catastrophizing, the absolutist language, the melodramatic predictions that would make Shakespeare think "wow, that's a bit much."

- Be specific. "I'm anxious" isn't helpful. "I'm convinced I'll bomb this interview, never get a job in my field, disappoint my family, and end up broke and alone living in a cardboard box under a bridge where even the pigeons will judge me" gives you something concrete to work with.

- Don't censor or judge. This isn't for anyone else to read. Let the irrational, embarrassing thoughts come out in their full, unfiltered glory, like finally admitting you've never actually seen The Godfather despite nodding knowingly whenever someone makes a reference to it.

3. **Look at it like a scientist studying a bizarre new species.** Now that it's external to you, examine it with curiosity rather than fear:

    - Is this 100% true? Or are there parts that are assumptions, exaggerations, or predictions that haven't happened yet and probably never will, like your brain's weather forecast that always predicts catastrophic hurricanes regardless of the season?

    - Do I have real proof? What evidence supports this thought, and what evidence contradicts it? Would this hold up in a court of law, or would the judge throw it out while rolling their eyes theatrically?

    - Is there a more balanced way to see this? If my best friend told me they were thinking this, what might I point out to them? Would I call them ridiculous or offer them compassion? (Hint: It's probably the second one, unless your friendship style is unusually brutal.)

    - What cognitive distortions am I using? Is there catastrophizing, mind-reading, fortune-telling, or black-and-white thinking happening here? Is my brain delivering these thoughts while wearing a flowing robe and carrying a crystal ball?

4. **Write a counter-thought next to it.** Create a more balanced perspective based on your analysis:

    - "I'm going to fail" to "I've succeeded before, and I'll do my best. Even if this doesn't go perfectly, one setback doesn't define me any more than that one time I walked into a glass door defines my ability to navigate physical spaces."

- "Nobody likes me" to "I literally have friends. Some people clearly enjoy my company. My brain is being melodramatic and overinterpreting limited data, like a statistician who makes predictions based on a sample size of exactly one person."

- "I'll never figure this out" to "Learning takes time. Feeling confused now doesn't mean I'll feel confused forever. I've learned complicated things before, like how to use a new phone without throwing the old one out the window in frustration."

- "This is going to be a disaster" to "Most things I worry about never happen. Even if challenges arise, I have resources and skills to handle them. I've survived 100% of my worst days so far, which is an impressive track record."

Anxious thoughts hate being written down more than vampires hate garlic-flavored sunlight. They thrive in the abstract realm of feeling and wither under the concrete scrutiny of language.

Because once you see them clearly, they lose their power. They transform from overwhelming emotional experiences to words on a page—words that can be questioned, analyzed, and reframed into something that actually serves you rather than paralyzes you.

Psychology Note: Try keeping an "anxiety journal" for a week. Write down your anxious thoughts as they occur, then come back to them later and analyze them. You'll likely notice patterns—the same core fears appearing in different disguises like villains in Scooby-Doo, the same catastrophic predictions that never materialize, the same distortions that cloud your thinking in predictable ways. This awareness alone can significantly reduce anxiety's grip, like realizing the "ghost" in your house is just that one pipe that makes weird noises when the heat comes on.

Step 2: Saying It Out Loud (Because Your Thoughts Sound Less Scary in Your Own Voice Than in Your Inner Darth Vader Voice)

Writing things down is great, but saying them out loud? That's next-level, like upgrading from a flip phone to a smartphone.

Because when you say an anxious thought out loud, in your normal voice—it almost immediately sounds ridiculous, like hearing your elaborate excuse for being late played back on a recording.

Your brain delivers thoughts in a very overreactiontic, doomsday narrator kind of way. Inside your head, even minor concerns can sound like they're being narrated by the voice from movie trailers: "IN A WORLD where you sent that text with a period instead of an exclamation point... NOTHING WILL EVER BE THE SAME. One woman's punctuation choice will DEVASTATE RELATIONSHIPS and DESTROY FUTURES. Coming this summer to a brain near you: 'PERIOD OF DOOM.'"

But when you say them out loud, they lose that scary, echoey, "voice of absolute truth" quality. They're just words, spoken in your ordinary human voice, subject to the same scrutiny as any other statement, like "I think I left the oven on" or "These pants definitely still fit me."

They just sound... dumb. Or at least significantly less convincing than they did in the echo chamber of your mind, like realizing your "brilliant" 3 AM idea sounds considerably less impressive in the harsh light of day.

Why This Works

It engages different neural pathways. Speaking activates motor areas in your brain that aren't engaged when you're just thinking, which can help interrupt anxiety's hold, like changing the channel when a scary movie comes on.

It forces clarity. Vague, amorphous anxiety must be translated into specific statements, which immediately makes them more manageable. It's hard to say "I just feel like everything is terrible and something bad is going to happen somewhere at some point" out loud without immediately realizing how unhelpful that is.

It activates your rational mind. Hearing yourself say something outlandish often automatically triggers your critical thinking skills, like your brain suddenly sitting up and saying "Wait, did I just hear what I think I heard? Let me fact-check that."

It creates healthy distance. When you speak a thought aloud, it becomes something separate from you—an object in the world that you can examine rather than an experience that defines you, like the difference between being stuck in quicksand versus looking at quicksand from a safe distance.

Try This

The next time anxiety is spiraling in your head, stop. Find a private moment—your car, bathroom, empty house, wherever you can speak freely without making nearby strangers wonder if they should call someone.

Say the thought out loud exactly how it's playing in your mind. Don't soften it or make it more reasonable. If your brain is saying, "Everyone at that meeting noticed you stumbling over your words and now they all think you're completely incompetent and they're probably texting each other about it right now and creating a secret Slack channel called 'let's-laugh-at-this-idiot' where they share memes about your incompetence," say exactly that.

Now, say it again in the most melodramatic, over-the-top voice you can. Exaggerate it to highlight its absurdity:

- Use a cartoon villain voice. "Muahahaha! Your career is DOOMED because you stuttered once! No one has EVER recovered from a verbal slip-up! NEVER! Soon, the entire professional world will know of your SHAME!" (Twirl imaginary mustache for extra effect)

- Use a Shakespearean tragedy voice. "Alas, poor professional! Thy reputation lies in tatters, destroyed by a single verbal misstep! What mortal can survive such a grievous wound to their credibility? O cruel fate! O wretched circumstance! Shall I compare thee to a day that really, really sucked?"

- Use a newscaster voice like you're reporting breaking news: "This just in: John Smith has just sent a text with no emoji. Experts say the recipient will hate him forever. The nation braces for the fallout. We go live to our correspondent at the scene of the empty text bubble. Sarah, what's the mood there?"

- Try a sports announcer: "Ohhh! And Smith fumbles the presentation! The crowd is silent! His career is going DOWN, folks! This could be the end of everything he's worked for! In all my years of broadcasting, I've never seen such a catastrophic use of 'um' in a professional setting! This will go down in the history books alongside the Titanic and New Coke!"

- Go with infomercial voice: "Are YOU tired of people RESPECTING you? Try our new product: Awkward Comment™! Just one application and you'll be replaying this moment in your head for YEARS TO COME! But WAIT! There's MORE! Act now and we'll throw in Ruminating At 3 AM absolutely FREE!"

Listen to yourself as if you were hearing someone else say these things. Would you find these statements reasonable or extreme? Would you tell a friend to calm down if they expressed these worries to you, or would you immediately help them draft a resignation letter and start looking at underground bunkers?

Suddenly, it's not so terrifying anymore. It might even be kind of funny, like realizing the "horrifying creature" in your dark bedroom was just your coat hanging on the door.

Because when you change the way you say it, you change the way you see it. You transform it from an unquestionable truth to a statement that can be evaluated, challenged, and even mocked.

And once you can laugh at a thought? It has no power over you anymore. It's been downgraded from a threat to a joke, from something that controls you to something you control, like discovering the schoolyard bully is afraid of butterflies.

Insight: This technique works especially well for those repetitive anxious thoughts that you intellectually know are irrational but still feel emotionally compelling. Saying them out loud helps align your emotional response with your intellectual understanding by making the irrationality so obvious it can't be ignored, like finally seeing the optical illusion correctly.

Step 3: Laughing at It (Because Anxiety is a Terrible Comedian with the World's Worst Netflix Special)

Anxiety is deeply unoriginal. For all its overwhelming emotional impact, it's actually quite predictable and repetitive in its content. It's the guy at the party who keeps telling the same story about that one time in college, thinking it gets better with each retelling.

It runs the same tired material over and over again, but somehow, we keep taking it seriously. It's like a comedian with only three jokes who somehow keeps getting booked for shows despite having a one-star rating on Yelp.

If we treated anxiety like a bad stand-up comic, we'd walk out of the show. We'd demand new material or, at the very least, better delivery. We'd write scathing reviews saying, "0/10, would not recommend. Same recycled content as last time, delivery was overoverreactiontic, and the performer seemed desperate for attention."

So why do we let it run the same routines in our heads and act like they're brand-new, credible concerns? Why do we keep paying attention when it's just recycling the greatest hits of our insecurities? It's like having a streaming service that only plays the same three shows you don't even like, but you keep renewing your subscription anyway.

If your anxiety keeps telling you the same thing ("You're not good enough, what if they hate you, what if you embarrass yourself"), it's time to flip the script. Time to become the critic rather than the captive audience. Time to leave that one-star review and change the channel.

Why Humor Works Against Anxiety

It changes your physiological state. Laughter activates your parasympathetic nervous system—the opposite of the fight-or-flight response that anxiety triggers. It's like trying to be both freezing cold and burning hot at the same time—your body can't do both simultaneously.

It creates cognitive dissonance. It's very difficult to be both amused and terrified at the same time. Humor forces a perspective shift, like trying to maintain your balance while also falling down—one of them has to give.

It builds resilience. Being able to laugh at your fears is a sign of psychological flexibility and emotional strength. It's like mental jiu-jitsu—using the energy of the attack to defeat it.

It brings proportion. Humor relies on incongruity and exaggeration, which helps highlight when your anxious thoughts are out of proportion to reality, like using a ruler to measure what you thought was a monster under your bed and discovering it's just a sock.

Exaggerate the Thought Until It's Obviously Stupid.

Take what your anxiety is suggesting and push it to its most absurd logical conclusion, like following the GPS that says "turn right" directly into a lake:

If anxiety says, "You're going to mess up and people will think you're dumb," go further.

"Oh, you're right, anxiety. One small mistake and I will be BANISHED from society, doomed to live in the woods, forced to start a new civilization with squirrels as my only companions. I'll have to fashion a shelter from leaves and twigs, using only the wilderness survival skills I clearly don't have since I can't even handle this presentation. I'll become a legend—'Did you hear about that person who mispronounced 'specifically' once and now lives in the forest and talks to pinecones?' Scientists will study me from a distance, documenting the first known case of death by embarrassment."

"Absolutely. That one typo in my email is going to single-handedly ruin my career. In fact, they're probably creating a museum exhibit about history's worst typos right now, and mine will be the centerpiece. 'And here we have the infamous 'Regards' that accidentally became 'Retards'—notice the perfectly preserved look of horror on the sender's face when they realized what happened. Scholars believe this marked the beginning of the Great Professional Downfall of 2025.'"

If your anxiety says, "They didn't text back, they must hate me," take it further: "Yes, not only do they hate me, they've probably formed an international anti-me coalition. They're printing t-shirts with my face crossed out as we speak. There are billboards going up worldwide. The UN is holding an emergency session to discuss the threat I pose to global harmony. Breaking news alerts are interrupting regular programming: 'This just in: Local person sent two texts in a row without a response. President to address the nation at 9.'"

Give Your Anxious Voice a Ridiculous Persona.

Personify your anxiety as someone or something whose opinion you wouldn't take seriously:

- Maybe it's a bad TV villain twirling their mustache while tying you to the railroad tracks of doom. "Muahahaha! Soon your social life will be MINE, all MINE!"

- Maybe it's a panicked squirrel named Marvin running in circles, hoarding nuts for a catastrophe that never comes. "WE NEED MORE NUTS! THE END IS NEAR! WHY AREN'T YOU PANICKING? I'VE SEEN THINGS, MAN!"

- Maybe it's that one relative who always overreacts to everything, who treats a paper cut like it requires emergency surgery. "Oh. My. You have a PIMPLE? Have you updated your will? Should I call the priest?"

- Maybe it's a doomsday cult leader who keeps predicting the end of the world but has to keep revising the date when nothing happens. "The great social rejection is coming on Tuesday! Oh, Tuesday passed? I meant NEXT Tuesday. My calculations were off."

- Maybe it's a melomelodramatic weatherperson who treats every cloud like it's the storm of the century. "BREAKING: Slight chance of uneasy silence during conversation later today! Take cover! Stockpile small talk topics! This is not a drill!"

The next time your brain starts spiraling, imagine it's coming from that voice. "Oh, it's just Panic Squirrel Marvin again, storing up disasters for winter. Thanks, Marvin, but I think I'll be fine even if I did accidentally like that 3-year-old Instagram post while stalking my ex."

Ask Yourself, "Would This Make a Good Sitcom Plot?"

Most anxiety-inducing situations would be played for laughs in a comedy:

If your anxious thought sounds like the kind of misunderstanding they'd put in an episode of a comedy show, then maybe it's not as serious as your brain is making it.

"This is such a classic sitcom scenario. Character A sends a text, Character B doesn't respond right away, Character A spirals into increasingly elaborate theories about why, creates fake social media accounts to check if they've been blocked, drives by Character B's house three times, and then it turns out Character B was just in the shower. Cue laugh track and credits."

"If this were an episode of [your favorite sitcom], the main character would spend 22 minutes avoiding this person because of an imagined slight, creating increasingly elaborate disguises and diving behind potted plants, only to discover they had no idea anything was wrong and were actually planning a surprise party for them the whole time."

Create an Anxiety Nickname or Catchphrase

Give your anxiety a name or signature line that makes it less threatening:

"Oh, there goes Catastrophe Carl again, predicting the end of the world because someone looked at me funny in the elevator. Classic Carl!"

"That's just my anxiety's greatest hit: 'Everyone Secretly Hates Me.' It's like the 'Free Bird' of my insecurities—always making an appearance at the worst possible moment when I'm just trying to enjoy the party."

"Here we go with Disaster Theater, now playing in my brain for a limited time only. Tonight's feature: 'The Email That Ruined Everything' – as implausible as it is terrifying!"

When you recognize an anxious thought pattern, mentally announce it like a familiar TV show: "And now, the return of 'What If Everything Goes Terribly Wrong'—season 35, episode 412. Previously on 'What If Everything Goes Terribly Wrong,' I convinced myself that my slightly sweaty handshake would make me unemployable forever."

Anxiety hates being laughed at more than cats hate unexpected cucumber encounters. It wants to be taken seriously, to be treated as an authority on your life and your future. It wants you to believe that its warnings are crucial, its predictions accurate, its concerns valid—like a toddler insisting they're actually a dinosaur and need to be addressed as "Mr. T-Rex" at all times.

Because the second you laugh, you stop treating it like a threat. You've recategorized it from "important warning" to "ridiculous overreaction." You've taken back the power to interpret your own experience rather than letting anxiety define it for you, like taking the microphone away from the worst karaoke singer at the party.

Humor isn't about denying real problems or avoiding necessary action. It's about recognizing when your anxiety has crossed from helpful caution into unhelpful catastrophizing. It's about maintaining perspective when your brain is trying to convince you that minor setbacks are major catastrophes, like distinguishing between "I should prepare for this presentation" and "I should fake my own death to avoid this presentation."

Step 4: Sharing It (When You're Ready)

Once you've developed some skill at externalizing your anxious thoughts through writing, speaking, and humor, you might consider the ultimate form of externalization: sharing them with someone else.

This is an optional step, and it requires careful consideration of who you share with. Not everyone will respond with the understanding and validation you need. Some people have the emotional intelligence of a potato and will tell you to "just stop worrying" as if you hadn't thought of that brilliant strategy already. But when you find the right person—a trusted friend, a supportive family member, a therapist, or even an online community of people with similar experiences—sharing your anxious thoughts can be tremendously liberating, like finally admitting you've never seen Star Wars despite nodding along to references for years.

Why Sharing Works

It normalizes your experience. Discovering that other people have similar anxious thoughts can be immensely relieving. You're not broken; you're human. You're not uniquely flawed; you're part of the world's largest, least exclusive club: People With Weird Thoughts.

It brings new perspectives. Others can often see flaws in your anxious logic that you might miss, offering alternative interpretations you hadn't considered. "Oh, I didn't think of it that way" is anxiety's kryptonite.

It reduces shame. Anxiety thrives in isolation and secrecy, like mold growing in a dark, damp corner. Bringing it into the open reduces its power to make you feel like there's something wrong with you. It's the emotional equivalent of turning on the bathroom light and realizing that scary shape is just your towel hanging on the door.

It strengthens connections. Vulnerability, when met with understanding, deepens relationships and builds trust. There's nothing like the relief of saying "So I have this weird thought..." and having someone respond, "Oh man, ME TOO!" instead of slowly backing away.

How to Share Effectively

1. **Choose carefully.** Share with people who have demonstrated empathy and understanding, not those who tend to dismiss emotions or offer toxic positivity like "Just think happy thoughts!" or "It could be worse—you could be on fire!"

2. **Be specific about what you need.** Sometimes you want solutions, sometimes just validation. It's okay to say, "I just need you to listen while I vent about this ridiculous thought my brain keeps having" or "I'd like your perspective on this thinking pattern—am I missing something obvious here?"

3. **Start small.** You don't need to reveal your deepest anxieties all at once. Begin with thoughts that feel less vulnerable and work your way up as trust builds.

Start with "Sometimes I worry people are judging my laugh" before diving into "I'm convinced I'm fundamentally unlovable and everyone's just pretending to like me."

4. **Remember that reactions say more about others than about you.** If someone responds dismissively or judgmentally, that reflects their limitations, not the validity of your experience. Some people are emotional Roombas—they can only handle so much before they need to be emptied.

Psychology Note: Many people find that simply knowing they're not alone in their anxious thinking patterns makes those patterns easier to recognize and manage. Anxiety whispers that you're uniquely flawed; connection proves otherwise. It's like discovering that what you thought was your weird, embarrassing quirk is actually something millions of people experience, like talking to your plants or having elaborate conversations with your pet.

Your Thoughts Don't Belong in the Shadows (They're Not Vampires, Although They Do Suck Energy)

Anxious thoughts thrive in silence. They grow bigger when they stay locked inside your head, like mushrooms flourishing in a dark, damp environment. They gain power from secrecy and isolation, like scammers who don't want you to "tell anyone about this amazing opportunity."

But when you write them down, say them out loud, or laugh at them?

They shrink, like a balloon slowly deflating with a sad whistling sound.

They lose their grip, like a toddler finally releasing the candy they've been clutching in their sweaty hand for hours.

They go from being overwhelming and terrifying to small, manageable, and even kind of funny, like finding out the "ghost" haunting your house is just your roommate's cat knocking things over at 3 AM.

Think of it as turning on the lights to discover that the monster in your room is actually just a pile of laundry. The "monster" doesn't disappear entirely—the laundry is still there—but it's transformed into something ordinary that you can deal with rather than something frightening that paralyzes you. "Oh, it's just shirts and pants. I should probably fold those instead of having a panic attack about them."

So the next time your brain starts its usual anxious monologue like a movie villain who can't stop explaining their evil plan?

Drag those thoughts out into the light. Get them out of the echo chamber of your mind, where they can bounce around unchallenged, gaining size and momentum with each reverberation, like a rumor spreading through a small town.

Write them down. See how different they look in black and white, stripped of their emotional soundtrack and special effects. Say them out loud. Hear how different they sound in your actual voice, without the melodramatic reverb your brain adds. Make them ridiculous. Experience how different they feel when wrapped in humor, like dressing up your fears in clown costumes. If you're ready, share them. Discover how different they seem when met with understanding rather than when they're festering in isolation.

Because once you see them clearly, hear them out loud, or laugh at their ridiculousness...

They stop feeling so powerful. They stop feeling like The Truth and start feeling like what they actually are: just thoughts. Just electrical impulses in your brain. Just habits of mind that you've developed over time and can, with practice, change.

And that transformation—from overwhelming truth to manageable thought—is where freedom from anxiety begins. It's like realizing the prison door was actually unlocked the whole time, and you can just... walk out anytime you want. The view's much better out here.

Chapter 9: The Power of the Absurd

Laughing at Anxiety Might Just Be the Best Thing You Do Today (And Your Brain Will Hate It)

So, Why Does Humor Work So Well Against Anxiety?

Let's take a moment to talk about one of the most underrated tools in your anxiety toolkit: laughter.

I know what you're thinking: "Wait, are you telling me I should just laugh my anxiety away? Like it's a joke? Should I also try curing a shark attack with a band-aid?"

Well, kind of, yes. And here's why:

Humor is one of the most powerful weapons against anxiety, stress, and negative self-talk. Not because it makes everything better instantly (nothing short of a magic wand or prescription-strength amnesia could do that), but because it shifts your brain's focus from problem-solving mode to solution mode.

This isn't just feel-good advice I found on a coffee mug at Target. There's solid science behind it. Research in the field of psychoneuroimmunology (try saying that five times fast after a glass of wine) has shown that humor triggers physical changes in your body. When you laugh, your brain releases dopamine and endorphins—neurochemicals that create feelings of pleasure and well-being. At the same time, laughter reduces the levels of stress hormones like cortisol and adrenaline, which fuel your anxiety like premium gasoline in a sports car headed for a cliff.

Let's break this down:

1. Humor Distracts You From the Spiral

When you're anxious, your brain is locked in a loop, running on auto-pilot and focusing only on the worst possible scenario. It's basically a conspiracy theorist with a podcast, connecting dots that don't exist and building a case that would make even the most gullible person say, "That's a stretch." The more you feed it that energy, the bigger the problem becomes.

But humor? Humor interrupts that loop like your mom walking in during the climactic scene of a movie you definitely weren't allowed to watch.

Think of it like this switch:

Anxiety: "You're going to fail, everyone will hate you, your entire life is a mess, and by the way, everyone at that party three years ago is STILL talking about that weird thing you said."

Humor: "Hey, remember that time you tripped in front of everyone and then tried to make it look like a dance move? That was hilarious. Maybe you'll do that again. If you're going to fail, at least fail spectacularly enough to go viral."

When you make fun of your anxiety, you change the narrative. Instead of spiraling into doom like you're the main character in a Nordic crime theatrics, you've reframed it into something more manageable—maybe even a comedy.

Consider this real-life example:

James was preparing for a job interview at a company he desperately wanted to work for. As the day approached, his anxiety ramped up: "What if I blank out? What if they think I'm incompetent? What if I'm the worst candidate they've ever seen? What if they create a special file labeled 'Never Hire This Person Or Anyone Related To Them'?"

Instead of fighting these thoughts, he leaned into absurdity: "Yes, I'll definitely be the worst candidate they've ever seen. Maybe I'll set a new company record! They'll probably create a special award in my name for future terrible candidates. The 'James Memorial Trophy for Outstanding Achievement in Interview Disasters.' They'll hang my picture in their lobby with a red X through it."

The exaggeration made him laugh, breaking the tension and allowing him to prepare more effectively for what was ultimately just a conversation with other human beings who probably also had anxious moments before their own interviews.

2. Laughter Relaxes Your Body (Yes, Really, Not Just Something Your Yoga Teacher Made Up)

You probably already know that anxiety has a physical effect on your body:
- Tight muscles (like you're auditioning for the role of "statue" in the world's longest-running play)

- A racing heart (like you just chugged four espressos and then watched a horror movie)

- Tension (as if someone replaced all your muscles with guitar strings and is constantly tuning them)

- Shallow breathing (because apparently your lungs decided they're now part-time employees)

- Digestive discomfort (your stomach hosting its own version of Fight Club)

But did you know that laughter has a physical effect too?

It reduces muscle tension, lowers your heart rate, and can even release endorphins—the body's natural stress relievers. It's like a spa day for your nervous system, but free and you don't have to make uncomfortable small talk with a stranger rubbing essential oils on your back.

Think about the last time you had a genuine, full-body laugh—the kind where your stomach hurts and you might even snort a little (which then makes you laugh harder because now you're embarrassed about snorting, creating a beautiful cycle of increasingly undignified noises). Remember how your body felt afterward? Lighter. More relaxed. Maybe even a little tired in the best possible way, like you just had a fantastic workout without moving from your couch.

This happens because laughter:

- Increases oxygen intake, stimulating your heart, lungs, and muscles (basically giving your insides a mini vacation to the mountains)

- Activates your stress response initially, then quickly cools it down, leaving you feeling more relaxed (it's like tricking your body: "DANGER! Just kidding!")

- Stimulates circulation, which helps reduce muscle tension (giving your tight muscles permission to stop being such overachievers)

- Releases neuropeptides that fight stress and potentially boost immune function (like tiny internal bodyguards against anxiety)

So when you make an anxious thought into a joke, your body relaxes. Your mind follows. Anxiety's grip loosens. And suddenly, that thing you were freaking out about doesn't feel so scary anymore. It's like anxiety showed up to your party dressed as the Grim Reaper, but when you laugh, the costume falls off and it's just your weird neighbor underneath.

Dr. William Fry, a Stanford University psychiatrist who studied the physiological effects of laughter, found that laughing 100 times is equivalent to 10 minutes of rowing or jogging. It's like an internal workout that counters the physical symptoms of anxiety. Finally, a workout routine I can commit to—binge-watching comedy specials on Netflix.

3. Humor Turns You into the Boss of Your Thoughts

The more you laugh at your anxiety, the more you remind yourself that it does not control you.

You take away its power. You are in charge. You're the CEO, and anxiety is just that intern who keeps sending company-wide emails with terrible ideas.

This is a psychological concept called cognitive distancing—creating space between yourself and your thoughts. When you can laugh at anxious thoughts, you're essentially saying, "That's just a thought, not reality, and I don't have to believe everything I think, especially since my brain's greatest hits album seems to be exclusively terrible remixes of 'Everything Is Going Wrong' featuring 'You're Not Good Enough.'"

Imagine this:

Anxiety comes knocking on your door, like a little gremlin with a loudspeaker and a PowerPoint presentation titled "101 Reasons Why You Should Panic Right Now":

"You're about to embarrass yourself, everyone's judging you, this is a disaster! Also, remember that thing you said in third grade? That was super weird and everyone still remembers!"

Now, instead of hiding under the covers or allowing your mind to spiral into catastrophe, you respond:

"Really? You've been saying this for years and nothing's happened yet. Let's hear what you've got this time. Should I grab some popcorn? Maybe take notes? Rate your performance on a scale of 1-10? Because honestly, your material is getting stale. You need some new material if you want to keep this show running."

Your confidence and control grow when you treat anxiety like it's a bad stand-up comedian who's running out of material and keeps recycling the same three jokes about airplane food and dating apps.

This approach works because it helps you:
- Externalize anxiety (seeing it as separate from yourself, like that weird collection of sauce packets in your fridge that somehow multiplies when you're not looking)
- Create psychological distance from threatening thoughts (they're over there, you're over here, enjoying your life)
- Reduce the perceived importance of worry triggers (turning mountains back into the molehills they always were)
- Demonstrate to yourself that you can choose how to respond to anxiety (you're the director of this movie, not just an actor reading anxiety's terrible script)

A therapist I know encourages her clients to give their anxiety a ridiculous name and an equally ridiculous voice. One client named her anxiety "Lord Doom-a-lot" and imagined it speaking in a pompous British accent while wearing a monocle and twirling an elaborate mustache. Whenever anxious thoughts appeared, she'd hear them in that voice, which made it nearly impossible to take them seriously. "I say, you're going to be absolutely DREADFUL at that presentation tomorrow. Simply DREADFUL!" is much harder to believe than the same message delivered by your own inner voice.

4. Laughter Gives You Permission to Be Human

Humor gives you permission to be imperfect and reminds you that everyone messes up sometimes. We're all just primates with smartphones, pretending we know what we're doing.

Anxiety loves perfectionism. It thrives on the belief that if you don't get everything right, you've failed. It's the Simon Cowell of emotions, ready with a cutting remark and an eye roll. But humor? Humor says:

"Hey, it's okay to mess up. Actually, messing up is kind of funny. Remember when you sent that text to the wrong person? Classic you! Let's do more of that!"

I mean, life is messy. We're all just walking around with metaphorical toilet paper stuck to our metaphorical shoes sometimes. But when you can laugh at your own mistakes instead of drowning in self-doubt, you begin to realize that nobody has it all together. That friend with the perfect Instagram feed? They definitely have a junk drawer full of random cables they can't throw away because "what if I need that someday?" And they probably talk to their pets in a baby voice when nobody's around.

When you can laugh at yourself, you're practicing self-compassion through humor—acknowledging your humanity rather than demanding perfection. This is particularly powerful because anxiety and perfectionism often go hand in hand, creating a vicious cycle where:

- You set impossibly high standards (like expecting yourself to give a TED talk-quality presentation at every team meeting)

- You inevitably fall short sometimes (because you're human, not a perfectly programmed presentation robot)

- Falling short triggers anxiety ("Everyone noticed that slide transition was uneasy and now they think I'm incompetent!")

- Anxiety makes you set even higher standards to avoid failure ("Next time I need BETTER slides, MORE preparation, and possibly to develop MIND CONTROL so they can't judge me")

- The cycle continues (and you consider living in a cave away from all human contact)

Humor breaks this cycle by making it okay to be imperfect. It says, "Yep, I messed up. That's what humans do. We're basically sophisticated chimps who invented taxes and reality TV."

Example:

Let's say you're about to speak in front of a group of people, and anxiety's doing its usual thing:

"This is it. You'll mess up, everyone will think you're stupid, and they'll never listen to you again. Also, your hair looks weird today."

Now, picture yourself on stage, you misspeak a word, and your brain screams, "You've ruined everything! Abort mission! Fake a medical emergency and run!"

But then you smile, shrug, and say:

"Well, I guess I'll have to invent a new language on the fly. Bear with me, folks. In my new language, that word actually means 'I'm crushing this presentation despite what my anxiety is telling me right now.'"

And guess what? The room lightens up, the tension dissolves, and your anxiety? It freaking hates that. It's like watching a vampire confronted with garlic-flavored sunlight.

This is why some of the most effective public speakers deliberately incorporate self-deprecating humor or call attention to their mistakes. It doesn't just endear them to the audience—it disarms their own anxiety. It says, "Yes, I know I'm imperfect, and I'm completely okay with that. In fact, I'm going to point it out before you even notice it."

Step 1: Laugh at Your Anxiety (Because It's Not Invincible, It Just Has Really Good PR)

When anxiety shows up, imagine it as a bad comedian on stage trying too hard—someone who bought a "Comedy for Dummies" book yesterday and is now attempting an open mic night with material exclusively about how terrible you are.

Anxiety: "This is going to be a disaster!"

You: "Really? A disaster? On a scale from 'spilled coffee on my shirt' to 'actual apocalypse,' where exactly are we landing here? I can't wait to see how this one plays out. Should I start hoarding canned goods or just grab an extra napkin?"

The absurdity of anxiety becomes more obvious the moment you choose to laugh at it instead of believing it, like suddenly noticing your scary shadow on the wall is just your cat sitting on your head lamp.

Think about it: anxiety tends to catastrophize—taking minor concerns and blowing them up to apocalyptic proportions. When you step back and look at this tendency objectively, it's actually kind of ridiculous. Your brain is telling you that forgetting one line in a presentation will lead to immediate termination, social ostracism, and possibly the end of civilization as we know it. "And then the aliens will refuse to make contact with humanity because YOUR POWERPOINT HAD A TYPO!"

This catastrophizing is anxiety's superpower. But absurdity is yours. It's like anxiety shows up with a lightsaber, and you counter with jazz hands.

Action Steps:

Next time anxiety shows up, laugh at it.

Create a "mental comedy club."

Turn every "disaster" into a punchline.

Practice "catastrophe one-upmanship" with yourself

One client I worked with called this her "disaster escalation technique." When anxiety told her a first date might go badly, she'd respond: "You're right. It'll go so badly that my date will write a bestselling memoir about it, and I'll see my uncomfortableness overreactiontized in the inevitable Netflix adaptation starring Anne Hathaway as 'Woman Who Snorted While Laughing And Then Tried To Cover It Up By Fake Coughing For Three Minutes Straight.'"

Step 2: Use Humor as a Release Valve (Before Your Head Explodes From Pressure)

Sometimes, anxiety doesn't need to be "fixed"—it just needs to be released, like a pressure cooker that's about to turn your kitchen ceiling into abstract art.

Humor is one of the fastest ways to release the pressure. It's like emotional WD-40 for your stuck mental gears.

If anxiety's building up and you feel that familiar tightness in your chest (the one that feels like you're wearing an invisible corset that's two sizes too small), give yourself permission to laugh.

This relates to the concept of emotional regulation—the ability to manage and respond to emotional experiences in a healthy way. Humor acts as what psychologists call an "adaptive coping mechanism," helping you process and release emotional tension without suppressing it or becoming overwhelmed by it. It's like having an emotional release valve that doesn't involve screaming into your pillow or stress-eating an entire cheesecake.

Example:

Your brain: "You're going to bomb this presentation. Everyone is going to see you fail. They'll record it and it'll become the next viral sensation, but not in a good way."

You: "Okay, let's make this interesting. Should I wear a tutu while presenting, or is that too much? Maybe I should just embrace the potential disaster and go full performance art. If I'm going to fail, I might as well make it memorable. RELEASE THE CONFETTI CANNONS!"

It's silly. It's light-hearted. And it's exactly what your anxiety hates. It's like trying to have a serious conversation with someone who keeps making fart noises—eventually, you just can't maintain the gravity of the situation.

Humor loosens the grip of anxiety by turning your situation into something manageable and less serious. It's hard to be terrified of something you're actively mocking.

Here are some practical ways to use humor as a release valve:

Create an anxiety alter-ego

Use the rule of three

Create anxiety "commercials"

Mark Twain famously said, "Humor is tragedy plus time." But you don't have to wait for time to pass—you can choose to view your current struggles through a lens of humor right now. It's like time-traveling to the future when you'll laugh about this, but without needing a DeLorean or 1.21 gigawatts of power.

Step 3: Find Your Favorite Comedy (Because Sometimes You Need Professional Help—Just Not The Kind You Think)

If you're not in the mood to make your own jokes, find someone else's. Humor is a serious stress reliever—and sometimes, it's easier to laugh when someone else is doing the heavy lifting. Not everyone can be a comedian, but everyone can appreciate good comedy, just like not everyone can make a soufflé, but everyone can eat one.

The science behind this is fascinating. When you laugh at content created by others, you're activating what neuroscientists call "mirror neurons"—brain cells that respond both when you perform an action and when you see someone else perform that action. This means that watching or reading something funny creates a similar neurological response to experiencing something funny firsthand. It's like your brain is playing a neurological game of "Simon Says" with the comedian.

How to Use Humor to Manage Anxiety

Hang out with someone who makes you laugh.

Create a humor journal

Laughter releases stress and helps you disconnect from the spiral of anxious thinking. It's like hitting the reset button on your brain—except the button is shaped like a whoopee cushion.

Research by Dr. Lee Berk at Loma Linda University found that even the anticipation of laughter can decrease stress hormones. Just knowing you're about to watch a funny video can start to reduce anxiety before the laughing even begins. It's like how your dog gets excited when you pick up the leash, except instead of a walk, you're getting endorphins.

Humor Puts Anxiety in Its Place (The Corner, Wearing A Dunce Cap)

Here's the key: Humor doesn't make your anxiety go away—but it does make it manageable. It's like putting your anxiety in a ridiculous costume—it's still there, but it's a lot harder to take seriously when it's wearing a clown nose and oversized shoes.

When you laugh at the ridiculousness of your anxious thoughts, they lose their power over you. It's like discovering the scary monster under your bed is actually just a pile of laundry you forgot to put away. Still annoying, but not terrifying.

You go from being controlled by anxiety to being the one who gets to decide how much weight those thoughts should carry. "Thank you for your input, anxiety, but I'm going to file that under 'ridiculous overreactions' and move on with my day."

This shift in perspective is profound. It's the difference between being a prisoner of your anxiety and being its observer. And sometimes, the best way to observe something is to laugh at it, like watching a nature documentary where the predator trips and falls face-first into the mud.

Think about professional comedians for a moment. Many of them talk openly about their struggles with anxiety and depression. Comedy becomes not just their career but their coping mechanism—a way to transform pain into something shareable and even beautiful. As comedian Maria Bamford put it, "The thing I love about comedy is that it's a symptom of pain." It's emotional alchemy—turning psychological lead into gold, or at least into something that glitters under the spotlight.

Humor isn't just a distraction from anxiety—it's a transformation of it. A reclassification from "threat" to "material." From "crisis" to "punchline." From "my life is over" to "this will make a great story someday."

So the next time your anxiety shows up uninvited like that relative who always crashes on your couch and eats all your food, don't try to force it away. Instead, laugh in its face. Offer it a seat and ask if it's considered a career in stand-up comedy, because its catastrophic thinking would kill at open mic night.

And then watch as it shrinks, confused by your reaction, like a bully who expected tears but got a witty comeback instead.

Remember: Anxiety wants you to take it seriously. It demands gravity and respect. It insists that every worry is a five-alarm fire requiring all emergency services and possibly the National Guard.

But you? You can choose to see the absurdity in it all. You can choose to laugh. You can say, "Nice try, anxiety, but that catastrophe forecast is about as accurate as a weather prediction two weeks out."

And that might be the most powerful choice you make today. Even more powerful than your choice of breakfast cereal, which, let's be honest, was a pretty big deal too.

PART 4: LONG-TERM THINKING – CHANGING YOUR INNER MONOLOGUE FOR GOOD

Now let's zoom out to the big picture: how to create lasting change in that noisy head of yours. In these final chapters, we'll tackle how to rewrite your core beliefs for good, the life-changing magic of not taking yourself so seriously (spoiler: you're not that important, and that's actually great news), and the ultimate freedom that comes from realizing you are not your thoughts. This isn't about quick fixes or temporary relief—it's about completely revamping your relationship with your mind for the long haul. Think of it as renovating your mental house from the foundation up, not just rearranging the furniture and hoping it looks better. By the time we're done, you'll be the boss of your brain instead of letting it boss you around.

Chapter 10: Rewriting Your Mental Script (For Real This Time)

Your Brain is Just an Old Google Doc. Time to Edit (And Delete Those Embarrassing Comments from 2014 That Make You Cringe Harder Than Your Middle School Photos)

Your Inner Monologue is Not Set in Stone (It's More Like a Bad Karaoke Track You Can Switch Off Before You Butcher Another Adele Song)

Picture this.

You're at a party. Someone tells a joke, and you try to add your own funny comment. Except—crickets. Not just any crickets, but crickets that seem to have microphones and amplifiers. No one laughs. The conversation moves on like a train that didn't bother to stop at your station because your station wasn't deemed worthy of being on the route map.

And suddenly, your brain slams the "self-destruct" button with the enthusiasm of a game show contestant who's been waiting all their life for this moment, rehearsing in their bathroom mirror while brushing their teeth.

"Oh no. That was so clumsy. Why did I say that? Everyone thinks I'm weird. They're going to remember this forever, like that time I called my teacher 'Mom' in third grade. They're probably creating a group chat right now just to discuss how unfunny you are. Look, that person just checked their phone—they're definitely adding to the 'Why We Don't Invite You Places' thread. I should never speak again. In fact, I should develop a mysterious illness that requires me to communicate exclusively through interpretive dance and silent movie title cards."

Never mind that no one reacted strangely. Never mind that people probably forgot about it five seconds later because they were too busy thinking about their own lives and wondering if their own joke from earlier bombed harder than a straight-to-streaming movie sequel. Never mind that everyone else at the party is just as neurotic as you are, just with different flavors of neurosis, like different Ben & Jerry's ice cream varieties of

CHAPTER 10: REWRITING YOUR MENTAL SCRIPT (FOR REAL THIS TIME)   133

social anxiety—from "Chunky Imposter Syndrome" to "Cherry Garcia's Fear of Public Speaking."

Your brain? It just filed this moment under: "Evidence That You're Awkward and Should Not Be Allowed to Speak in Public, Ever, Including at Drive-Thrus and Self-Checkout Machines That Ask If You Found Everything Okay."

And that's how the script gets written.

Not by some objective, truth-based system created by an impartial committee of reasonable observers with fancy clipboards, but by random moments that your brain decides to blow out of proportion like a movie director with an unlimited special effects budget and something to prove to their ex who said they'd never make it in Hollywood.

Your inner monologue—the running commentary in your head that makes sports announcers seem quiet and restrained by comparison—wasn't something you chose, like your Netflix watchlist (which, let's be honest, you also don't choose very well because who actually watches those documentaries you add?).

It was built over time, shaped by experiences, mistakes, criticism, and random social situations where your brain decided, "Yep. Let's hold on to that forever. In fact, let's replay it at 3 AM ten years from now when you're trying to sleep before an important meeting, right after we remind you of that weird thing you said to your crush in high school and right before we make you wonder if you locked the front door even though you checked three times."

But here's the thing:

What If Your Brain Has Been Running on an Outdated Script This Whole Time? (Like Using a MapQuest Printout in the Age of GPS)

Think about it.

If a movie script is bad, what happens? They rewrite it. Even massive franchises with zillion-dollar budgets still do reshoots when the dialogue isn't working. They don't just shrug and say, "Well, I guess audiences will have to suffer through Superhero Man saying 'My greatest power is the power of love' without irony."

If a novel needs editing, what happens? The author revises it, sometimes so drastically that the final version barely resembles the first draft. Stephen King doesn't publish his first thoughts at 2 AM after too much coffee.

If your phone has outdated software, what do you do? You update it, because nobody wants to be that person still using iOS 7 and having their apps crash every time they try to post a picture of their lunch, which, let's face it, nobody wanted to see anyway.

So why—WHY—do we just assume that the thoughts in our head are final, unchangeable, and set in stone? Why do we treat our mental narratives like they were handed down on tablets from a mountain, instead of what they really are: a collection of half-baked conclusions drawn by our prehistoric monkey brains during moments of stress or embarrassment, like a conspiracy theorist connecting random events on a corkboard with red string and thumbtacks?

Your thoughts? They are just words. Words you wouldn't even let a mediocre middle school poet get away with at an open mic night where the only other performers are the host's relatives.

Your beliefs? They are just habits. Like biting your nails or scrolling Instagram on the toilet, but less visible to others (thank goodness—imagine if people could see your thoughts while you're in a boring meeting pretending to pay attention).

Your inner voice? It's just a script. And not even a good one—we're talking straight-to-streaming bad, not awards-season contender. We're talking eighth sequel in a franchise that should have stopped after the second movie.

And here's the best part:

You can rewrite it. You can be the ruthless editor your mental screenplay desperately needs. The Simon Cowell of your own brain, but with better hair and less unnecessarily mean comments about people's dreams.

This isn't about fake positivity or "just think happy thoughts" while you twirl in a meadow pretending your problems don't exist like you're in a medication commercial.

This is about actively challenging the garbage scripts your brain has been feeding you and replacing them with something better. Something that actually passed a basic fact-check. Something that wouldn't make you roll your eyes if you heard someone else say it at a dinner party, making you wonder how they function with such poor critical thinking skills.

Let's get to work. Grab your red pen—we've got some serious editing to do. Your brain's screenplay has been in development hell long enough.

Step 1: Identify Your Core Script (What Have You Been Telling Yourself, You Poor Thing With a Brain Like That?)

Your brain has a core script—the thoughts that play on repeat, quietly shaping how you see yourself. It's like having an earworm, but instead of "Baby Shark," it's "You're Not Good Enough: The Extended Dance Remix featuring DJ Anxiety and MC Self-Doubt" playing at full volume at 3 AM.

To find yours, ask yourself:

- What's the first thing you think when you mess up? (Besides "Where's the nearest hole I can crawl into?" or "Is faking my own death an overreaction to forgetting to attach the file to an email?")

- What do you assume people think about you? (Mind reading: the superpower nobody asked for but everyone thinks they have, right up there with "ability to pick the slowest line at Trader Joe's every single time.")

- What are the thoughts that come up when you feel anxious or insecure? (Your brain's greatest hits album of terrible remixes, now with bonus catastrophizing! Available wherever intrusive thoughts are sold!)

Most of us have one or two negative scripts that pop up over and over, like that friend who keeps telling the same story at every gathering because they got a laugh once in 2016 and have been chasing that high ever since.

Common examples:

- **"I'm not good enough."** (Compared to what? A hypothetical perfect version of yourself that doesn't actually exist? Your Instagram feed at 2 AM when everyone else seems to be on vacation in Bali while you're eating cereal for dinner?)

- **"I always mess things up."** (Always? Really? Even breathing? Blinking? Existing in Earth's gravitational field? Your ability to consistently find the bathroom when needed suggests otherwise.)

- **"Nobody really likes me."** (Not even your dog? That barista who smiles at you? The delivery person who you've built an entire imaginary friendship with based on the fact that they once said "nice weather" to you? Your mom's friend who still likes all your Facebook posts from 2012?)

- **"I'll never get my life together."** (Because clearly, you can see the future, and it exclusively contains mismatched socks and expired yogurt. Your crystal ball must be working overtime to deliver such specific disappointments.)

These scripts often originate from specific experiences in our past. Perhaps a teacher once told you that you weren't creative, or maybe you were rejected by someone important to you, or you failed at something that mattered deeply. Your brain took that single event and generalized it into a universal truth about your identity with the logical reasoning skills of a conspiracy theorist with a podcast and too much free time.

For instance, that time in fourth grade when you froze during your oral report might have created the script "I'm terrible at public speaking," even though you were just nine years old and nervous, as any child would be when forced to stand in front of 25 other tiny judgmental humans who were waiting for you to mess up so they could have something to talk about at recess. Or maybe you made a calculation error at work last year, and your brain decided this means "I'm bad with numbers" rather than "I made a mistake that one time because I was trying to calculate percentages while also listening to a true crime podcast and eating hot soup, like the reckless multitasker I am."

If one of these hits a little too close to home, congrats—you've just found the faulty script your brain has been running. It's like discovering your car's GPS has been directing you to drive through lakes because it hasn't been updated since 2007 and thinks that new subdivision is still a river.

Now let's fix it before you metaphorically drive into another lake based on outdated mental mapping.

Step 2: Challenge the Script Using CBT Techniques (Where Your Brain Gets Cross-Examined Like It's on Law & Order: Special Thoughts Unit)

Your brain loves to make bold, overreactiontic statements with zero supporting evidence. It's basically a Twitter account with no fact-checkers, operating at 3 AM after too many energy drinks.

CHAPTER 10: REWRITING YOUR MENTAL SCRIPT (FOR REAL THIS TIME)

So let's apply Cognitive Behavioral Therapy (CBT) techniques to challenge those thoughts. Think of this as putting your brain on the witness stand and asking, "Where's your evidence, buddy? Show me the receipts."

CBT is one of the most evidence-based approaches to changing thought patterns. It's been studied extensively and shown to be effective for anxiety, depression, and various forms of negative thinking. The fundamental principle behind CBT is simple but powerful: by examining and challenging our thoughts, we can change how we feel and behave. It's like being your own personal detective, but instead of solving crimes, you're solving the mystery of why your brain is being such a jerk when you're just trying to live your life and enjoy your coffee in peace.

1. The Thought Record Method (AKA: Fact-Checking Your Brain's Fake News Network)

This is one of the most effective CBT techniques for changing negative self-talk. It's like forcing your brain to show its work on a math problem instead of just shouting "The answer is you're terrible!" and running away.

Let's say your script is: "I'm not good enough."

Write down these four things:

The Thought: "I'm not good enough."

The Evidence For It: (Spoiler: There's usually not much beyond "because I said so" energy.)

- "I made a mistake last week."

- "I sometimes feel like I don't measure up."

- "I didn't get the promotion I wanted."

- "My soufflé collapsed that one time in 2019 and Gordon Ramsay wasn't even there to yell at me about it."

The Evidence Against It: (Time to fight back with the fury of someone defending their favorite TV show's controversial final season online!)

- "I've succeeded before."

- "I've been complimented on my work."

- "Not feeling good enough doesn't mean it's true, just like feeling like I could win a dance battle against a professional doesn't make that true either."

- "I've overcome challenges in the past."

- "My friends and family value me."

- "I have unique skills and perspectives that others appreciate."

- "I can make a really good sandwich. Like, restaurant-quality good. The kind people would pay actual money for."

- "That one coworker always asks me for help with Excel formulas, which means I know something someone else doesn't."

A More Balanced Thought:

- "Sometimes I doubt myself, but I have proof that I'm capable, even if my brain is being selective with its memories like it's creating a true crime documentary where I'm the villain."

- "I am learning and growing—I don't have to be perfect. Nobody starts out great at anything except maybe crying and pooping, and I've already mastered those skills as a baby."

- "Making mistakes doesn't mean I'm not good enough; it means I'm human, not a robot. Even robots make mistakes, which is why Captcha tests exist."

- "My worth isn't determined by a single outcome or another person's judgment. If it were, we'd all be doomed by that one person who decided mullets should make a comeback."

- "Even Beyoncé has off days, although hers probably still look better than my best days, but that's beside the point."

Let's look at a real-life example:

Situation: You give a presentation at work and stumble over your words a few times.

Automatic Thought: "I'm terrible at public speaking. Everyone probably thinks I'm incompetent. They're all texting each other about how bad it was right now. I should probably update my resume and look into living in a remote cabin where I never have to speak to anyone again except maybe squirrels."

Evidence For:
- "I did stumble over my words."
- "I felt nervous."
- "I saw someone check their phone during my talk."
- "I said 'um' approximately 7,432 times."
- "I momentarily forgot what slide I was on and just stared at the screen like I was trying to decode ancient hieroglyphics."

Evidence Against:
- "Several people nodded in agreement during key points."
- "My boss specifically thanked me afterward."
- "I received thoughtful questions, showing people were engaged."
- "I've given successful presentations in the past."
- "Everyone gets nervous sometimes."
- "The person checking their phone might have been responding to an urgent message about their child's school or their dying plant at home or maybe they were actually taking notes on my brilliant points."
- "Nobody ran screaming from the room or fell asleep with their eyes open."

Balanced Thought: "While I wasn't perfectly smooth in my delivery, the content was solid and people were engaged. Public speaking makes most people nervous, and I can continue to improve with practice. Being nervous doesn't mean I'm incompetent. Also, Steve Jobs himself flubbed presentations sometimes, and he did okay for himself. And if TikTok has taught us anything, it's that people make mistakes on camera all the time and still manage to have careers and followers."

Do this whenever a negative thought pops up. It's like having a bouncer at the door of your mind, checking IDs and not letting in thoughts that can't provide proper identification. "Sorry, 'I'm a total failure,' your evidence is too flimsy. Back of the line."

Because the more you challenge it, the weaker that script gets. It's like facing a playground bully—once you stand up to it, it tends to back down and go pick on someone else. Your negative thought is basically the mental equivalent of a bully who secretly has very low self-esteem but a very loud voice.

2. The Courtroom Method (Where Your Thoughts Get Put on Trial in the People's Court of Your Mind)

This technique treats your negative thought like a witness in court. Except in this courtroom, you get to be the prosecutor, the defense attorney, AND the judge. It's like a one-person production of "Law & Order: Special Thoughts Unit" where the only commercial breaks are when you get distracted by your phone notifications.

Let's put "I'll never get my life together" on trial.

Prosecutor (your anxious brain): "Your Honor, my client's life is a mess. Look at all the things they haven't figured out yet. They're behind on their career goals, their apartment is disorganized, and they still don't know what they want to do long-term. Everyone else seems to have it figured out by now. Their former classmate is already a VP, and they're still trying to figure out how to properly fold a fitted sheet and why their succulents keep dying despite allegedly being 'impossible to kill.'"

Defense Attorney (your rational brain): "Objection! My client has made progress. They've handled things before. They paid off their student loans ahead of schedule. They've maintained meaningful friendships for years. They recently learned to cook three new healthy meals. They are actively working on themselves by reading this book and applying these concepts, which most people aren't doing while binge-watching 'Real Housewives' debates about who threw wine at whom.

And the claim that 'everyone else has it figured out' is hearsay and inadmissible—most people are figuring things out as they go, they're just not posting about their existential crises on Instagram. They're posting carefully filtered photos of their brunches instead. Also, nobody knows how to fold fitted sheets. Nobody. That's why linen closets have doors. And Marie Kondo makes millions of dollars teaching people to just roll things up and call it a day."

Judge (you, the final decision-maker): "The evidence for 'never getting life together' is weak and based on selective attention to struggles while ignoring accomplishments. Case dismissed. The revised verdict: 'I'm working on different aspects of my life at different paces, just like everyone else. Also, I'm going to buy storage bins for those fitted sheets because some battles aren't worth fighting.'"

This method helps you step back from emotions and look at your thoughts objectively. It introduces a crucial element of psychological distance that allows you to see your thoughts as separate from your identity. You're not your thoughts; you're the person observing your thoughts, like watching particularly overreactiontic squirrels in a park fighting over an acorn like it's the last piece of food on earth.

Consider another example:

Thought on Trial: "I'm a failure as a parent."

Prosecutor: "Your child is struggling in math, and you lost your temper when helping with homework last night. Good parents don't lose their temper. You're basically creating a supervillain origin story here. Twenty years from now, your child will be in therapy saying, 'It all started when my parent couldn't explain fractions without sighing dramatically.'"

Defense: "My client has consistently shown up for their child in countless ways—attending school events, providing emotional support, teaching values, and creating a loving home. They apologized after losing their temper and modeled how to take responsibility. No parent is perfect 100% of the time, and research shows that repair after mistakes is what matters most in parenting. Even the parents on those perfect-looking family Instagram accounts lose their cool sometimes—they just stop filming when it happens and only post the parts where everyone is laughing while making organic slime together."

Judge: "The charge of 'failure as a parent' is dismissed. The evidence shows normal human imperfection within the context of consistent care and responsibility. Court awards the defendant one self-compassion break and permission to order takeout tonight. Also, YouTube tutorials for math help are hereby admissible as parenting tools."

3. The "Would You Say This to a Friend?" Test (Exposing Your Double Standards Like a Reality TV Show Host)

If your best friend came to you and said:

"I'm such a failure. I'll never figure things out. My life is a dumpster fire with particularly toxic smoke. The kind where authorities evacuate the neighborhood."

Would you say:

"Yep. You're doomed. Give up now. Have you considered living in a cave? I hear Tasmania has nice ones. Maybe start practicing your bat impersonation."

No. You would not say this unless you're secretly a villain in a Disney movie or a Netflix reality show contestant who "didn't come here to make friends."

More likely, you'd say something like: "That's not true at all. Remember how you handled that difficult situation last month? And you've made so much progress on your goals this year. Everyone feels lost sometimes, but that doesn't mean you are a failure. You're just going through a tough patch. Here, have some chocolate and let's figure this out together while watching that show where attractive people compete to date someone they've never seen."

So if you wouldn't say it to someone else, why are you saying it to yourself? Why does your internal dialogue sound like it's being written by your meanest middle school bully after they found out you had a crush on someone who doesn't know you exist?

This test exposes how unfair and harsh your inner voice can be. It reveals that you're essentially running a weird double standard where everyone else deserves compassion and understanding, but you deserve a constant stream of criticism delivered by a drill sergeant with a megaphone who follows you even into the bathroom.

Flip the script: Talk to yourself like you would talk to someone you love. Or at least like you'd talk to a coworker you respect but don't know well enough to be brutally honest with about their questionable lunch choices.

Try this exercise: Write down three things you've been telling yourself lately. Then imagine your closest friend said these exact same things about themselves. Write down what advice you would give them. Now, read that advice back to yourself. Feel the cognitive dissonance wash over you like a wave of "oh, I see what you did there, brain, you sneaky little self-saboteur."

For example:

What you tell yourself: "I'm so stupid for making that mistake at work. I should probably be working at a carnival guessing people's weights instead of having a professional job."

What you'd tell a friend: "Making a mistake doesn't make you stupid. Everyone makes mistakes, especially when they're learning something new or under pressure. What matters is how you handle it and what you learn from it. Remember last month when our boss made that huge error in the presentation? We didn't think he was stupid—we recognized he was human. You deserve that same grace. Plus, carnival weight-guessers actually use complex visual assessment techniques, so that's not even a good insult."

What you tell yourself: "No one wants to hear what I have to say. My opinions are about as valuable as a screen door on a submarine."

What you'd tell a friend: "That's not true! Your perspective is valuable and unique. Not everyone will connect with your ideas, but that doesn't mean they aren't worth sharing. The right people will appreciate what you have to offer. Remember when you made that suggestion in the meeting last week? The whole team built on it. Your voice matters. And honestly, a screen door on a submarine would be great when it's parked at the dock and the crew wants some fresh air without mosquitoes getting in."

Now apply that same compassionate perspective to yourself. It might feel strange at first, like wearing someone else's shoes that don't quite fit, but with practice, it becomes more natural. Eventually, you'll stop emotionally beating yourself up for the crime of being an imperfect human in an imperfect world where even Instagram models get pimples and have bad hair days they don't post about.

Step 3: Rewrite the Script with a CBT-Based Counterstatement (Your Brain's Extreme Makeover: Thought Edition)

Now, let's create new, better scripts. Think of it as a mental renovation—tearing out the outdated, depressing wallpaper of your thoughts and replacing it with something that doesn't make you want to move out of your own head and sublet it to someone with better decorating sense.

The most effective rewrites aren't just positive affirmations where you chant "I am amazing" into the mirror until your neighbors call for a wellness check and your cat looks at you with judgy eyes. They're balanced statements that acknowledge reality while removing the harsh, absolutist language that makes negative thoughts so damaging.

Here's a simple formula:

Old Thought: "I'm not good enough." **New Thought:** "I have strengths and weaknesses like everyone else, but I am learning and improving. Also, 'good enough' is a moving target that not even Olympic athletes can consistently hit. Even Simone Biles falls sometimes, and she can literally fly."

Old Thought: "Nobody likes me." **New Thought:** "I may feel insecure sometimes, but I have people who care about me. Not everyone will connect with me, and that's normal. Even Keanu Reeves probably has people who think he's overrated, though they're objectively wrong and should reconsider their life choices."

Old Thought: "I always mess things up." **New Thought:** "I've made mistakes, but I've also had successes. One mistake doesn't define me or predict my future performance. If I actually messed up 'always,' I'd be a statistical anomaly worthy of scientific study. Scientists would be fighting to interview me about my perfect record of imperfection."

Old Thought: "I'll never be as successful as others." **New Thought:** "Everyone's path is different. I'm making progress in my own way and on my own timeline. Comparing my journey to others' doesn't serve me. Also, social media is basically a highlight reel of people's lives, not the blooper reel they don't share. For all I know, that 'successful' person from high school cries in their car before work while eating gas station taquitos."

Old Thought: "I'm too anxious to handle this situation." **New Thought:** "I feel anxious right now, but I've handled difficult feelings before. I can take this one step at a time. Anxiety is an uninvited party guest, not the host. I can acknowledge it's here without letting it control the music and eat all the good snacks."

The key is balance.

You're not lying to yourself—you're just choosing a healthier, more accurate thought. The goal isn't to convince yourself that everything is perfect or that you never make mistakes. The goal is to see yourself and your situations clearly, without the distortion of overly negative interpretations, like cleaning a smudged pair of glasses you've been wearing for years and suddenly realizing that what you thought was an ugly bird is actually just your attractive neighbor.

Notice that these rewrites:

- Acknowledge the feeling without accepting it as fact (like saying "I feel cold" instead of "This room is freezing"—one is your experience, the other is a debatable claim that your office mate with the personal space heater will definitely fight you on)

- Introduce nuance where the original thought was absolute (because real life rarely fits into simplistic categories, except maybe "foods that combine well with cheese" and "foods that don't")

- Recognize your capacity for growth and change (because you're not a statue, you're a work in progress, more like a garden that needs regular tending than a finished sculpture)

- Consider evidence that contradicts the negative belief (because your brain is terrific at cherry-picking the bad and ignoring the good, like a toddler who only eats the marshmallows out of Lucky Charms)

Step 4: Practice Until It Feels Real (Fake It Till You Remake It, Like a Pop Star Reinventing Their Image)

At first, these new thoughts will feel weird. Like wearing someone else's clothes or calling your teacher "Mom" in elementary school, prompting that horrifying slow-motion moment of realization as the entire class turns to stare at you.

That's because your brain has been running the old script for years. It's comfy with it. It's like that ancient, ratty sweatshirt you should have thrown out years ago but still wear around the house because it's "broken in," even though your partner has threatened to "accidentally" lose it during the next move.

Think about it like learning a new language—at first, the words feel foreign and uncomfortable. You have to consciously translate everything. But with consistent practice, it starts to feel more natural. Eventually, you can think in that new language without effort. You're no longer translating—you're just speaking. You've gone from "where is the biblioteca" to dreaming in Spanish.

But the more you repeat them, the stronger they become.

Think of it like muscle memory:

The first time you question a thought, it's hard. Like trying to do a push-up after years of your only exercise being reaching for the remote and arguing with your smart TV when it doesn't understand your voice commands.

The tenth time? Easier. Like that push-up after a few weeks of training, when your arms no longer feel like overcooked spaghetti.

The hundredth time? It's automatic. You're the push-up champion of your block and don't even think about it anymore. You're basically the mental equivalent of someone who casually mentions their marathon time in unrelated conversations.

Here are some practical ways to reinforce your new scripts:

Morning mental rehearsal: Spend two minutes each morning deliberately practicing your new thoughts. Imagine situations that would normally trigger your old script, and mentally rehearse responding with your new, balanced thoughts. Like a fire drill, but for your brain. "In case of self-criticism, break glass and retrieve balanced perspective."

Physical reminders: Put sticky notes with your new scripts in places you'll see them regularly—your bathroom mirror, your desk, or as a lockscreen on your phone. Subtle ones work too, so your coworkers don't start asking questions about the "I AM NOT A FAILURE" Post-it on your computer monitor, leading to awkward conversations at the coffee machine.

Accountability partners: Share your old and new scripts with someone you trust. Ask them to gently point out when you slip into old thinking patterns. "Hey, I think you're doing that thing again where you assume everyone at this party is secretly judging your laugh that sounds like a dolphin being tickled."

Trigger identification: Notice the specific situations, people, or environments that tend to activate your negative scripts. Being aware of these triggers gives you a chance to prepare your new thoughts in advance. "Family holiday dinner? Time to prep my mental armor against Aunt Judy's comments about my career choices, relationship status, and apparent failure to appreciate her special cranberry sauce recipe from 1973."

Schedule check-ins: Set a recurring calendar reminder to assess how often you're using your new scripts versus falling back on old ones. This helps you track your progress over time. Treat your thought patterns like a project with KPIs (Key Performance Indicators) that you can monitor. "Self-criticism is down 27% this quarter, while reasonable self-assessment is up 32%. The board will be pleased."

This is cognitive restructuring.

It's how you train your brain to think differently. Like teaching an old dog new tricks, except you're both the dog and the trainer, and the trick is being kinder to yourself while still acknowledging reality. It's not about turning into a delusional optimist who thinks everything is amazing when it's clearly not—it's about not being a delusional pessimist who thinks everything is terrible when it's clearly not.

And over time? Your entire inner monologue shifts. The voice in your head starts sounding less like a critic and more like a coach. Less Simon Cowell, more Ted Lasso.

Consider this real-life example:

Sarah had always thought of herself as "bad with money" after making some financial mistakes in her twenties. This script led her to avoid looking at her bank account (the financial equivalent of covering your ears and humming loudly while shouting "LA LA LA I CAN'T HEAR YOU"), which only made her financial situation worse, like ignoring a leaky pipe until your ceiling collapses during a dinner party.

When she started challenging this thought, she felt like an impostor. "Who am I kidding?" she thought. "I've always been terrible with money. My potted plants have better financial skills than I do, and they don't even have bank accounts or opposable thumbs." But she persisted, replacing "I'm bad with money" with "I've made financial mistakes in the past, but I can learn to make better decisions now."

The first time she sat down to create a budget, her old script screamed loudly like a toddler denied candy in the checkout line. The tenth time, it was more of a whisper, like that same toddler when they're trying to stay up past bedtime but are clearly about to pass out. After a few months of consistent practice—setting up automatic savings, tracking expenses, and celebrating small wins—she realized she hadn't thought "I'm bad with money" in weeks. The new script had become her default. Now when she looks at her bank account, she thinks, "I'm managing my money," not "I'm messing up my money like it's my job and I'm up for employee of the month."

You Are the Narrator, Not the Script (Be Morgan Freeman, Not an Extra Who Gets Two Lines Before Being Eaten by the Monster)

Right now, your brain might be running an old, unhelpful script that makes you doubt yourself, overthink everything, and assume the worst. It's like having a pessimistic sportscaster narrating your every move: "And once again, they've chosen the slowest line at the grocery store. This continues their lifelong streak of poor decision-making. Let's watch that failure in slow motion while I point out everything they could have done differently, starting with their choice of breakfast cereal this morning."

But that script?

It's not permanent. It's not carved into stone tablets. It's more like something written in dry-erase marker that you've just never bothered to wipe away because you thought it was permanent marker and now you're too embarrassed to admit you were wrong.

You can challenge it. Like a lawyer poking holes in a flimsy argument while making dramatic gestures in front of the jury.

You can edit it. Like a ruthless book editor cutting unnecessary chapters that add nothing to the plot except confusion and boredom.

You can rewrite it entirely. Like a showrunner who decides to take the series in a completely new direction for season two after reading all the negative Twitter reactions to season one.

Chapter 11: The Life-Changing Magic

Relax, You're Not That Important—And That's a Good Thing.

Your Brain Is Running an Old Script—Time for a Rewrite

Your brain has been recording and replaying scripts from childhood, social interactions, and past failures like it's creating the world's most depressing Spotify playlist. And without asking your permission, it's been playing them on repeat at full volume at 3 AM when you're just trying to sleep.

This is where Neuro-Linguistic Programming (NLP) comes in—not just as a fancy psychological term, but as your personal brain-rewiring toolkit. NLP explores the critical connection between your neurology, language, and behavioral patterns. It's based on the revolutionary idea that you can systematically change how your brain processes information by altering the language patterns you use internally.

Right now, if you take yourself way too seriously, it's because your brain is running default scripts like:

- "If I mess up, people will reject me faster than streaming services cancel good shows."

- "I have to be perfect or I'll be exposed as the fraud I secretly believe I am."

- "If I don't succeed at this specific thing, my entire identity is worthless."

These aren't random thoughts—they're sophisticated neural pathways that have been reinforced over years, creating what NLP calls your "mental map" of reality. And here's the kicker: your map is not the territory. It's just your interpretation of it.

The Neural-Linguistic Connection: Why Your Brain Believes Its Own Bull

Your brain doesn't just randomly generate anxiety—it follows specific linguistic patterns that trigger predictable neurological responses. When you tell yourself, "I always mess things up," your nervous system responds as if this were an objective fact rather than a heavily biased interpretation.

This is where NLP's meta-model comes in—a framework for identifying and challenging these distorted language patterns. Every time you use absolutes like "always," "never," or "everyone," you're programming your brain to ignore contradictory evidence. Your nervous system can't tell the difference between a real threat and one you've linguistically constructed.

When you say, "Everyone will judge me if I speak up," your amygdala activates as if you're facing actual social rejection. Your palms sweat, your heart races, and suddenly you're in fight-or-flight mode over a completely imaginary scenario you've created through language.

How NLP Rewires Your Brain's Response System

NLP isn't just positive thinking—it's strategic reprogramming of your neural pathways through precise language interventions. Here's how to actually implement it:

1. Meta-Model Questioning: Challenging Your Brain's Faulty Logic

The meta-model in NLP identifies specific language patterns that distort reality. Learning to recognize and challenge these patterns is like installing a lie detector for your own thoughts.

When your brain says: "I'm going to bomb this presentation and everyone will think I'm incompetent."

Challenge it with these meta-model questions:
- "Everyone? Who specifically would think that?"

- "What evidence do you have that you'll 'bomb' it?"

- "How exactly would you measure 'bombing' versus just being imperfect?"

These questions force your brain to move from vague catastrophizing to specific, testable hypotheses—which almost always reveals the absurdity of your fears.

PSYCHOLOGY INSIGHT: Next time anxiety hits, write down exactly what your brain is saying, then circle all the absolutes, mind-reading assumptions, and predictions. For each one, ask: "How do I know this for certain?" Watch your brain stutter as it tries to justify its catastrophic forecasts.

2. Submodality Shifts: Changing How Memories Feel

One of NLP's most powerful techniques involves manipulating the sensory qualities of your internal experiences. Every memory or thought has specific "submodalities"—visual, auditory, and kinesthetic characteristics that determine its emotional impact.

Anxious thoughts tend to be:

- Visually large, close, and bright

- Auditorily loud with a harsh tone

- Kinesthetically intense and overwhelming

PRACTICAL NOTE: Try this submodality intervention:

1. Identify an anxious thought about yourself

2. Notice its current submodalities (size, brightness, volume, location)

3. Systematically alter these qualities:

   - Shrink the image down to thumbnail size

   - Push it 20 feet away from you

   - Turn down its volume to a whisper

   - Change its color to something ridiculous (hot pink?)

   - Add a silly soundtrack (maybe circus music?)

This isn't just visualization—it's rewiring how your brain stores and accesses this information. Research shows these interventions actually change the neural firing patterns associated with these thoughts.

When a critical thought appears, try saying: "Let me adjust the settings on this thought" and deliberately modify its sensory qualities until it loses its emotional charge.

3. Anchoring: Installing Psychological Power Buttons

Anchoring in NLP is far more sophisticated than just thinking happy thoughts. It's about creating deliberate neurological associations between specific stimuli and resourceful states—effectively installing "activation buttons" for confidence, calm, or clarity.

The science behind anchoring involves neural coupling—when neurons that fire together wire together. Here's how to create anchors that actually work:

1. Choose a unique physical trigger (e.g., pressing your thumb and middle finger together in a specific way)

2. Recall a time when you felt exceptionally confident—not just the memory, but the full-body sensation

3. At the peak of this state, apply your trigger for 5-10 seconds

4. Break state completely (think about something neutral)

5. Repeat this process 5-7 times with different memories but the same resourceful state

6. Test your anchor by applying the trigger and noticing the state change

For maximum effectiveness, stack multiple anchors by sequentially activating different confidence memories while maintaining the trigger. This creates a composite neural pathway that's significantly stronger than a single association.

KEY INSIGHT: The key difference between amateur and effective anchoring is specificity and repetition. Vague states like "feeling good" won't anchor well—you need precise, intense emotional states paired with unique triggers.

4. Linguistic Presuppositions: The Hidden Commands in Language

NLP has identified linguistic patterns that bypass conscious resistance and directly program your brain. These "presuppositions" are embedded assumptions that your brain accepts without question.

Instead of saying: "I hope I don't mess this up," (which presupposes messing up is likely)

Try: "I wonder how quickly I'll feel comfortable once I start speaking," (which presupposes you will feel comfortable—the only question is how soon)

Other powerful presupposition patterns:

- "Before you feel completely confident, you might notice your breathing becoming calmer" (presupposes confidence is coming)

- "As you continue developing this skill..." (presupposes continued improvement)

- "Which part of this presentation will you enjoy delivering most?" (presupposes enjoyment)

Your brain processes these embedded commands without the resistance it might offer to direct statements. It's like sneaking past the bouncer at the club of your subconscious.

PRACTICAL APPLICATION: Practice rewriting your anxiety-inducing self-talk using these patterns. Instead of "Don't panic," try "As you continue feeling more at ease, you might notice your shoulders relaxing."

5. Perceptual Positions: Hacking Your Own Perspective

One of NLP's most transformative frameworks involves deliberately shifting between different perceptual positions:

- First position: Your own perspective

- Second position: Another person's perspective

- Third position: An objective observer's perspective

When you're caught in self-criticism, systematically move through these positions:

1. First position: Notice your thoughts and feelings about the situation

2. Second position: Step into the shoes of others involved—how might they actually see this situation?

3. Third position: Imagine watching this scene as a compassionate observer—what would they notice about everyone involved?

This isn't just perspective-taking—it's training your brain to recognize that your initial interpretation is just one of many possible views, and often the least objective one.

NLP TIP: When worried about a social interaction, try asking: "If I were observing this situation as a neutral third party, what would I actually see happening here?" This creates immediate psychological distance from your anxiety.

Neural Reprogramming: From Self-Criticism to Self-Mastery

Perhaps the most powerful NLP insight is that your brain responds to imagined experiences almost identically to real ones. This means you can systematically rehearse new responses to triggers that usually send you into a spiral.

The New Behavior Generator technique:

1. Identify a situation where you typically overthink or become self-critical

2. Visualize watching yourself handling this situation with ideal responses

3. Now step into that visualization and experience it first-person

4. Run through this scenario multiple times, making adjustments until it feels natural

5. Add a distinctive anchor to this new behavioral pattern

This isn't wishful thinking—it's creating new neural pathways before you need them. Olympic athletes use similar techniques, with brain scans showing that mental rehearsal activates many of the same neural circuits as physical practice.

DAILY PRACTICE: When facing a challenging situation, take 30 seconds to run a mental simulation of your ideal response. Your brain will recognize this as a familiar pattern rather than defaulting to its catastrophic programming.

Your Brain Is Trainable, Not Fixed

NLP's core premise is revolutionary: your brain's responses aren't fixed—they're learned patterns that can be systematically redesigned. Taking yourself too seriously isn't an inherent personality trait; it's a specific neural program running on outdated information.

The next time your brain starts its familiar scripts of self-importance or catastrophizing, remember: you're not stuck with your current mental software. You have the tools to rewrite the code.

Nobody is watching your every move. Nobody is keeping track of your uneasy moments in a leather-bound journal titled "Evidence That You're a Disaster." Most people are too busy worrying about their own perceived disasters to catalog yours.

Life is a whole lot easier when you stop taking yourself so seriously. You're not the center of the universe—and thank goodness for that. What a relief to be just another person doing their best, making mistakes, learning, and moving on.

Reframe it. Interrupt it. Anchor a new response. Move on.

Because ultimately, the most serious thing you can do is lighten up.

Chapter 12: The Final Word – You're Not Your Thoughts

Just Because Your Brain Says It, Doesn't Mean It's True.

Mindfulness: The Art of Not Taking the Bait

Your brain is like a clickbait news feed run by a teenager with an energy drink addiction and unlimited WiFi. It throws out attention-grabbing headlines all day long:

"You're probably failing at life right now! Click to see why!"

"Nobody actually likes you—they're just being polite! Exclusive footage inside!"

"That weird thing you said last week? Yep, they're still thinking about it and have told at least 17 other people!"

The problem? You keep clicking on the headlines like they're offering free pizza instead of emotional torture. Then you wonder why you feel like garbage wrapped in anxiety sprinkled with dread.

Mindfulness teaches you how to stop clicking. It's learning to say, "Interesting headline, Brain FM, but I think I'll pass on that story today. I have better things to do than attend your catastrophe convention."

Mindfulness is not about clearing your mind or sitting in silence for an hour while your legs go numb and you contemplate your life choices. It's about learning to observe your thoughts instead of being dragged around by them like a person being pulled by an enthusiastic but untrained Great Dane on a leash through a squirrel sanctuary.

How Delusions of Reference Trick You into Thinking Everything is About You

Ever walked into a room and thought everyone was looking at you like you're a celebrity who just crashed a small-town wedding wearing a meat dress?

Or felt like people were secretly talking about you in that meeting, even though they were probably discussing their weekend plans or that new show on Netflix they're all obsessed with but you haven't started yet?

That's called a delusion of reference—a cognitive distortion where your brain assumes random events are about you when they're absolutely not. It's like thinking the universe is a reality show and you're the star, when actually you're just an extra getting coffee in the background of scene 47.

Your brain is like an overzealous TV writer with a deadline and seventeen espressos, trying to insert you into every storyline: "Those people laughed when you walked by? Obviously about your hair! That text went unanswered for 20 minutes? They're drafting a formal letter of friendship termination with their lawyer!"

But mindfulness teaches you how to step back and see reality for what it is—a world where most people are too wrapped up in their own plotlines to be writing yours. They're all starring in their own shows, where they're the anxious protagonist wondering if YOU noticed THEIR clumsy laugh.

How Mindfulness Helps You Stop Overreacting to Your Thoughts (A.K.A. The "Please Shut Up, Brain" Toolkit)

1. Thought Labeling: Call It What It Is

The moment you name a thought, it loses power over you faster than a vampire in sunlight holding garlic bread.

"I'm probably going to mess this up." → Label it: "Ah, there's my old friend, fear of failure. Right on schedule. Almost didn't recognize you without your PowerPoint of past embarrassments."

"They haven't texted back. They must be mad." → Label it: "Oh hello, classic overthinking. I was wondering when you'd show up today. Did you bring your jump-to-conclusions mat?"

"Everyone at this party is judging my outfit." → Label it: "There's that spotlight effect again, making me think I'm the main character when everyone else is too busy worrying about their own outfit choices."

When you label thoughts instead of believing them, you create distance between you and them. You're not having thoughts—you're watching them perform their little anxiety theater in the corner while you get on with your day.

PRACTICAL TOOL: The "I Am Not My Thoughts" Journal

Keep a small notebook with three columns:

1. The thought that's hijacking your brain

2. The label or category it belongs to (catastrophizing, mind-reading, fortune-telling)

3. What's actually happening in reality right now

After a week, you'll start to see patterns that make your internal critic as predictable as a rom-com plot.

Try saying: "I notice I'm having the thought that..." before your worry. It's like putting your anxious thought in quotes or giving it air quotes with your fingers—instantly less believable, like when someone says they're "totally fine" after dropping their phone in the toilet.

2. The "Movie Screen" Method (Or: Becoming the World's Chillest Film Critic)

Instead of getting caught in your thoughts like they're quicksand, picture them playing on a movie screen at a theater where you're just a casual viewer who can leave anytime—not the director, producer, AND main character with your career on the line.

- See the thought appear on the screen: "What if I get fired tomorrow?"

- Notice the genre: "Ah, this is clearly from the 'Catastrophic Future' collection. Very dramatic. Poor lighting. Unconvincing plot."

- Observe it like a passing cloud or a bad commercial between shows: "Interesting plot development, but the character motivation seems thin."

- Let it float away as the next thought-scene plays, without feeling the need to write a review or see how it ends.

PRACTICAL TOOL: The 30-Second Movie Trailer

When anxiety hits, set a timer for 30 seconds. During that time, imagine your anxious scenario playing out as a ridiculous movie trailer with an over-the-top voiceover: "In a world where one uncomfortable comment at lunch could ruin EVERYTHING... One person faces the ultimate challenge: getting through Tuesday." When the timer ends, the preview's over. Back to regular programming.

Not every thought needs a reaction, a response, or a five-paragraph essay analyzing its implications. Some can just be background noise while you focus on what you're actually doing—like those terms and conditions you scroll past without reading. ("I hereby agree that my brain can catastrophize occasionally without me buying into it...")

When anxiety shows up with "What if they're all judging me?", try: "Thanks for that fascinating screenplay, Brain. I'll file it under 'Speculative Fiction' and get back to my actual life now. Your Academy Award for Most Dramatic Interpretation of Basic Social Interaction is in the mail."

3. The 5-Second Grounding Trick (Because Sometimes You Need an Emergency Ejection Button)

When your brain is in panic mode running disaster simulations like it's getting paid overtime with holiday bonuses, bring it back to the present using your senses faster than clicking your heels three times while saying "there's no place like calm."

PRACTICAL TOOL: The 5-4-3-2-1 Sensory Reset

- 5 things you can SEE: "I see my coffee mug, my keyboard, that weird stain on the ceiling I've been ignoring, my plant that's somehow still alive, and my cat judging me silently."

- 4 things you can TOUCH: "I feel my chair beneath me, my sweater against my skin, the cool surface of my desk, and my hair that desperately needs washing."

- 3 things you can HEAR: "I hear the hum of the refrigerator, someone's muffled conversation outside, and my own breathing that's finally slowing down."

- 2 things you can SMELL: "I smell coffee and the lavender candle I bought to seem like someone who has their life together."

- 1 thing you can TASTE: "I taste the mint from my gum/toothpaste/questionable lunch choice."

Your anxious brain is like a time traveler stuck between regrettable pasts and apocalyptic futures. Grounding yanks it back to the present moment—the only time you actually have any power. It's like grabbing your brain by the shoulders and saying, "HELLO? WE LIVE HERE, IN THIS MOMENT, WHERE THINGS ARE ACTUALLY FINE."

BONUS MICRO-PRACTICE: The 3-Breath Reset

Whenever you feel your brain spinning into anxiety orbit, take three deliberate breaths:

1. First breath: Notice you're spinning out (awareness)

2. Second breath: Feel your feet on the ground (grounding)

3. Third breath: Decide where to put your attention now (redirection)

This takes about 10 seconds and can be done anywhere—in meetings, at dinner with your in-laws, or while your friend is telling you about their crypto investments for the 47th time.

4. The "What If... So What?" Strategy (A.K.A. Taking the Power Back from Your Worst-Case Scenarios)

Your anxious thoughts love the phrase "What if..." more than teenagers love saying "literally" and "like" in the same sentence while rolling their eyes.

"What if I mess up this presentation and everyone thinks I'm incompetent?" "What if they're mad at me and the friendship is ruined forever?" "What if this physical symptom means I'm dying instead of just having too much caffeine?"

Here's how you respond like the mindfulness ninja you're becoming:

PRACTICAL TOOL: The Worst-Case Scenario Survivalist Guide

1. Follow the fear to its ridiculous conclusion: "Okay, I mess up the presentation. Then what? People judge me. Then what? Some might think I'm not prepared. Then what? I might not get picked for the next project. Then what? Life... continues anyway?"

2. Flip the question: "What if it actually goes well? What if I nail this presentation? What if they're not mad at all and were just busy because not everything revolves around me and my anxiety?"

3. Reality-check your survival odds: "Have I survived embarrassment before? Yes, approximately 3,427 times. Will I survive this too? Probably, unless my embarrassment has suddenly developed the ability to actually kill people, which seems unlikely."

4. Plan one actual action step: "If I'm worried about the presentation, I'll practice the opening once more. Then I'll let it go, because over-rehearsing just gives my anxiety more time to throw a rager in my brain."

By making peace with the worst-case scenario, you take away its power like unplugging the TV during a scary movie. Plus, your brain's worst-case scenarios are usually about as realistic as a Hollywood disaster film where one person somehow saves the entire planet while maintaining perfect hair and finding love.

5. The RAIN Method: A Mindfulness Downpour for Thought Storms

When anxious thoughts are creating a category 5 hurricane in your mind, try the RAIN approach—which is less about weather and more about not drowning in your thoughts:

PRACTICAL TOOL: The RAIN Process (Your Personal Mental Weather System)

- R - Recognize what's happening: "I'm having anxious thoughts about this meeting. My palms are sweaty, knees weak, arms are heavy. Yes, I just quoted Eminem because my brain is that chaotic right now."

- A - Allow it to be there without fighting it: "These thoughts can hang out. I don't need to evict them or argue with them or throw them a going-away party. They can just be there like that weird chair in the corner of my room that I've been meaning to deal with for months."

- I - Investigate with kindness: "What's really behind this worry? Am I afraid of judgment? Rejection? That everyone will discover I'm making this up as I go along like everyone else on planet Earth? Interesting."

- N - Non-identification: "These thoughts aren't me—they're just mental weather passing through. I am not my anxiety any more than I am the song stuck in my head or that embarrassing memory from 7th grade that still pops up while I'm trying to sleep."

This is like being the meteorologist of your mind—you're reporting on the conditions, not personally experiencing every lightning bolt. "Today's mental forecast includes scattered anxieties with a 60% chance of overthinking by afternoon, clearing up by evening when you remember none of this actually matters that much."

When your brain says "Everyone will laugh if you speak up in this meeting," respond with: "That's an interesting forecast, but I've noticed your prediction accuracy is worse than a weather app during monsoon season. I'll wait and see what actually happens instead of trusting your dramatic interpretation."

6. The Body Check-In: Because Your Body Is Trying to Tell You Things

Your body is like that friend who knows you're stressed before you do—the one who says "You seem tense" right before you snap at someone for breathing too loudly.

PRACTICAL TOOL: The 60-Second Body Scan

Set a timer for one minute (yes, just one—this isn't a spa day) and move your attention through your body:

1. Start at your feet: Are they tense? Relaxed? Tap them on the floor to wake them up.

2. Move to your legs: Are they crossed? Bouncing? Still? Notice without changing.

3. Check your belly: Is it tight? Is your breathing shallow? Take one deeper breath.

4. Notice your shoulders: Are they making friends with your ears? Gently roll them down.

5. Finally, your jaw: Are you clenching it like it owes you money? Relax it slightly.

This quick scan helps you notice where you're physically holding tension—because anxiety isn't just mental gymnastics, it's also your body running a marathon while sitting still. Fun!

When you find tension, try saying: "I notice my shoulders are tight right now, and that's okay. They can relax a bit if they want to." Talk to your body like it's a nervous pet—gentle, kind, and slightly amused by its melodramatic reactions.

7. The "Name It to Tame It" Emotion Labeling Technique

Your emotions are like toddlers throwing tantrums in a grocery store—ignoring them just makes them scream louder, but acknowledging them can sometimes magically calm them down.

PRACTICAL TOOL: The Emotion Vocabulary Expander
Instead of just feeling "bad" or "stressed," get specific:
- "I'm feeling disappointed that my plan fell through"
- "This is frustration because things are moving slowly"
- "I'm experiencing anticipatory anxiety about this conversation"

Being precise does two things: it gives your analytical brain something to do besides panic, and it downgrades giant, vague emotions into smaller, more manageable ones. It's the difference between "I'm DYING of hunger" and "I could use a snack."

Studies show that simply naming your emotions reduces their intensity in your brain. It's like saying "I see you there, anxiety" instead of becoming anxiety's unwilling host body as it puppets you through your day.

Try this daily for a week: Set three random alarms on your phone. When they go off, name whatever emotion you're feeling in that moment with the most specific word you can find. Bonus points for using words like "peeved," "disgruntled," or "mildly bemused" instead of the usual suspects.

How to Train Your Brain to Stop Freaking Out Over Nothing (The Daily Mental Workout Plan)

Not every thought deserves your attention, just like not every social media notification needs an immediate response, and not every ex deserves a response to their "hey stranger" text at 1 AM.

You control the volume of anxious thoughts—they might be playing, but you have the remote. And yes, you can hit mute sometimes.

You can reset your nervous system at any moment; it's not stuck on "panic mode" permanently. Your body isn't a Windows computer from 1998—you don't have to just sit there and watch it freeze.

Practice these mindfulness skills daily—not just when you're already in meltdown mode. It's like building a muscle; you don't start weightlifting only when you need to move a couch. By then, it's too late and you'll probably hurt yourself and end up ordering pizza for the friend who actually helped you move.

DAILY MINDFULNESS MICRO-PRACTICES (For People Who Cannot Sit Still to Save Their Lives):

1. **The Toothbrush Meditation**: While brushing your teeth (which you hopefully do daily), focus ONLY on the sensation of brushing. When your mind wanders to your to-do list or what that person meant by "interesting" in their email, gently bring it back to the brushing. Bonus: your dentist will think you've finally listened to them about proper brushing time.

2. **The Traffic Light Reset**: Every time you hit a red light, take three deep breaths instead of checking your phone. Green means go back to your regularly scheduled overthinking. This works with elevator rides and microwave countdowns too.

3. **The Notification Pause**: Before checking any notification on your phone, take a single breath. That's it. Just one breath between the stimulus (ding!) and your response (immediate dopamine-seeking behavior). You might find half the notifications aren't worth the breath you just took.

4. **The "What's Not Wrong Right Now" Game**: When anxiety spikes, ask yourself: "What's actually NOT wrong right now?" Maybe your coffee is still warm. Maybe your favorite song is playing. Maybe your body is functioning reasonably well. Find five things that aren't currently disasters.

5. **The Mindful Bite**: Take the first bite of one meal each day with complete attention. No phone, no TV, no mentally rehearsing conversations. Just you and your food having a brief but meaningful relationship. Notice the texture, temperature, and taste like you're a food critic who gets paid by the adjective.

Try setting "mindfulness triggers" throughout your day:

- Every time you wash your hands, take three mindful breaths (bonus: you'll avoid those pesky respiratory infections AND anxiety spirals)

- When you receive a text, pause for 2 seconds before checking it (revolutionary concept, I know)

- Each time you walk through a doorway, notice your thoughts without judging them (doorways as mental checkpoints—who knew architecture could be therapeutic?)

- Whenever you take a sip of water, feel the sensation of swallowing (suddenly hydration becomes meditation—efficient!)

These tiny practices build your "noticing muscles" so when anxiety shows up with its breaking news alert about how everything is terrible and it's probably your fault, you're already trained to see it as just another broadcast you can choose to ignore like those extended warranty calls about your car.

8. The Self-Compassion Emergency Kit

Here's something your anxiety doesn't want you to know: you're allowed to be kind to yourself when you're struggling. Revolutionary concept, I know.

PRACTICAL TOOL: The Three-Part Self-Compassion Lifeline

When your thoughts are being particularly cruel, try this three-step approach:

1. **Mindfulness**: "I'm noticing I'm having some really harsh thoughts right now." (Not "I'm a disaster" but "I'm noticing thoughts about being a disaster"—gentle but crucial difference)

2. **Common Humanity**: "Literally millions of people are having similar thoughts right now. We're all in this weird human experience together, freaking out about things that probably won't happen while ignoring the good stuff right in front of us."

3. **Self-Kindness**: "What would I say to a friend feeling this way?" (Spoiler: probably not "you're right, you ARE a failure who should hide forever.")

Then actually say that kind thing to yourself, either in your head or out loud if you're alone and want to really commit to the bit. Something like "This is hard right now, but you're doing your best with what you've got. Also, your hair looks fantastic today."

Self-compassion isn't self-indulgence—it's recognizing that being human is complicated and messy, and treating yourself like you matter anyway. Wild concept, I know.

Final Thought: You Are Not Your Thoughts—You Are the One Watching Them

Your brain will always have something to say, like that one friend who can't handle silence in a car ride and starts telling you about their cousin's neighbor's weird toe collection. But now? Now you know how to respond.

When that anxious narrator starts broadcasting again? Turn the volume down. Change the channel. Move on with your day like the main character of your life who finally realized they don't have to listen to every thought that passes through their head.

Because you are the one in control now—not the panicked news station your brain thinks it's running. You're the viewer with the remote, and sometimes the best thing you can do is hit "mute" or switch to a channel that isn't running 24/7 disaster coverage of your life.

And remember: Having anxious thoughts doesn't make you an anxious person any more than standing in a garage makes you a car, or owning yoga pants makes you someone who actually does yoga. You're the sky, and thoughts are just weather passing through. Sometimes it's sunny, sometimes it's storming, but the sky remains.

Now go practice some mindfulness before your brain convinces you that mindfulness is too hard and you should probably just scroll through social media instead to see what everyone else is doing better than you. That narrator is sneaky, but you're sneakier. You've got this—even on the days when it feels like you don't.

And hey, if you forget everything else in this book, remember this: Your thoughts are just suggestions, not commands. You get to decide which ones deserve your attention and which ones should be left on read like that ex who only texts when they're lonely.

Welcome to mindfulness—the art of not believing everything your brain tells you. The view from here is much nicer, I promise. You've learned a lot about how to talk back. And now? Now you know when to talk back, how to talk back, and—perhaps most importantly—when to just ignore your brain entirely and let it ramble like an old man yelling at pigeons. Your brain will be absolutely shook by your newfound confidence. It'll throw out its best hits—catastrophizing, self-doubt, "what if" spirals—just waiting for you to take the bait. But this time? You know better. This time, you get to decide which thoughts deserve airtime. This time, when Skippy the Anxiety Gremlin starts up, you'll roll your eyes and say, "Oh, we're doing this again? Cute." And instead of spiraling, you'll switch the station. Because at the end of the day, talking back isn't just about silencing anxiety—it's about reclaiming control. You are not your thoughts. You are the one listening to them. And now, you finally know how to respond. So go ahead, talk back. For real this time.

A Letter to All the Overthinkers

Well, look at you. You made it to the end of this book.

And unless someone forced you to read this (which, if so, please blink twice for help), that means you've been on a journey inside your own head—which, let's be honest, is the most exhausting, unpredictable, plot-twisting place you could possibly explore. Like visiting Disney World, but instead of Mickey Mouse, you're greeted by your childhood embarrassments wearing name tags.

You've spent years living with a narrator that replays your mistakes in HD, catastrophizes random situations, and occasionally convinces you that mild inconveniences are actually signs of the apocalypse. Your brain is basically a conspiracy theorist with a podcast called "Everything Is Terrible And Here's Why: Episode 4,387."

And now? You know how to talk back.

That's a big deal. Like, "just learned to use the force" big deal.

Permission to Be Human

Before we wrap this up, let's get one thing straight: You're still going to overthink sometimes.

Yes, even after all this work. Even after learning how to challenge your thoughts, identify cognitive distortions (your brain's greatest hits album of terrible remixes), and tell Anxiety to take a seat. Not just any seat—the wobbly chair at the back of the classroom that nobody wants.

Why?

Because you're human, not a robot. (Unless this book is being read by future AI overlords, in which case—hi, please be nice to us, we're the ones who taught our toasters to love.)

Overthinking isn't something you just "fix" and never deal with again. You don't wake up one day and suddenly have a mind that only produces confident, well-adjusted, perfectly rational thoughts. (If you do, you might be a superhero, and we should talk. Also, can I borrow your cape?)

But here's the good news: You don't have to eliminate overthinking. You just have to stop letting it run the show. It's like having that one overreactiontic friend who always thinks the restaurant hostess hates them—they can still come to dinner, but they don't get to pick where everyone sits.

You've learned how to catch your thoughts before they spiral, challenge them before they wreck your day, and—most importantly—laugh at them before they convince you that you need to move to another country because you accidentally waved at someone who wasn't waving at you. (We've all been there. That person in the coffee shop is probably not still thinking about it. Probably.)

And that's the whole point. You don't have to stop overthinking. You just have to stop believing every ridiculous thing your brain throws at you. Your brain is like a toddler bringing you random objects: "Here's a leaf! Here's a rock! Here's a catastrophic interpretation of that text message that just means they're busy!"

The Best Habit You'll Ever Develop

Out of all the life skills you could master, learning how to talk back to yourself is one of the most valuable.

Because every single day, for the rest of your life, you will wake up with your own thoughts. Your brain's morning routine is more consistent than your coffee habit.

Some of them will be helpful. ("Maybe eat breakfast!")

Some of them will be neutral. ("That cloud looks like a duck.")

And some of them? Will be absolute garbage. ("Let's replay that embarrassing thing from third grade and feel bad about it right now!")

Your job isn't to stop them. Your job is to decide which ones deserve your attention. Like being a bouncer at the world's most chaotic club, but the club is your brain and everyone trying to get in is wearing a t-shirt that says "TOTAL DISASTER."

And now, you actually know how to do that.

So the next time your brain tries to convince you that one uncomfortable conversation has permanently ruined your social life? That you're now on some sort of universal blacklist of "People Who Said 'You Too' When the Movie Ticket Person Said 'Enjoy Your Film'"?

Talk back. "Thanks for the overreactiontic interpretation, brain, but I'm pretty sure they've already forgotten about it while I was still cringing in the hallway."

The next time Anxiety whispers, "Something bad is definitely going to happen," with zero supporting evidence? When it's sitting there like a cat that woke you up at 3am just to stare at you?

Talk back. "Cool theory. Got any evidence, or are we just making stuff up now? Because I can also make stuff up. Maybe something AMAZING is about to happen instead."

The next time your thoughts start spiraling into "I'm not good enough, I'll never figure this out, I'm probably a disaster of a human being who should be studied by scientists as an example of what not to do"?

Talk. Back. "Wow, that's quite the conclusion from forgetting to reply to one email. If forgetting things made people disasters, we'd all be walking catastrophes. Let's try again tomorrow."

Because you are not your thoughts.

You are not your mistakes.

You are not a walking collection of anxious spirals waiting to happen.

You are learning, growing, and doing the best you can with a brain that sometimes acts like it's being paid per worry.

And if you need a reminder?

Well, you just wrote yourself one. Look at you, being all prepared for future freak-outs. That's growth.

You're Doing Good, You're Better Than You Think

Here's the part where I could tell you to "just believe in yourself" or "think happy thoughts" or "trust the process."

But let's be real.

You probably overthink those phrases too. "What does 'trust the process' even MEAN? Which process? Who certified this process? Does the process have references?"

So instead, I'll leave you with this:

You are not alone in your overthinking. There's a whole army of us out there, silently rehearsing conversations that will never happen.

You are not failing just because you have bad mental habits. That's like saying you're failing at being human because you occasionally trip over nothing.

You are allowed to mess up, learn, and try again. Your brain's not a performance art piece—it's a work in progress.

You are way more capable than your brain gives you credit for. If your thoughts were Yelp reviews, they'd be the unreasonable ones complaining about the weather as if the restaurant controlled it.

And if you ever forget that?

You already know what to do.

Talk back.

www.ingramcontent.com/pod-product-compliance
Ingram Content Group UK Ltd.
Pitfield, Milton Keynes, MK11 3LW, UK
UKHW021311180426
11947UKWH00015B/1164

9 798992 958201